RELENTLESS
GROWTH

*How Silicon Valley Innovation
Strategies Can Work
in Your Business*

CHRISTOPHER MEYER

THE FREE PRESS

THE FREE PRESS
A Division of Simon & Schuster Inc.
1230 Avenue of the Americas
New York, NY 10020

Manufactured in the United States of America

10 9 8 7 6 5 4 3

Library of Congress Cataloging-in-Publication Data

Meyer, Christopher
  Relentless growth : how Silicon Valley innovation strategies can
work in your business / Christopher Meyer.
    p. cm.
  Includes bibliographical references and index.
  ISBN 0–684–83446–4
  1. Technological innovations—Management. 2. Corporations—
Growth—Management. 3. Semiconductor industry—California—Santa
Clara County. I. Title.
  HD45.M45 1997
  658.5'14—dc21   97–30740
                                                                   CIP

To Breckin for his top billing,
Frank for his music,
Adam for his enthusiasm,
and most important, Nancy,
for her unconditional love and affection

Contents

Foreword

For far too many firms, creating new products and services turns out to be a disappointing and unsatisfying undertaking—whether it involves generating new ideas and new concepts for an existing business, complementing a traditionally hardware-focused business with distinctive services and software, creating whole new businesses, or addressing new customer segments. Nevertheless, hope springs eternal, and most managers believe that if their organization could effectively innovate, they would indeed be able to get ahead of the game and grow profitably.

Yet at least one area of the industrial landscape, Northern California's Silicon Valley, has a large number of individuals, firms, and supporting organizations that understand and apply the principles leading to sustained patterns of innovation and growth. Obviously, not all Silicon Valley firms are successful, but for a significant number, growth in revenues, profits, and jobs, and a sustained pattern of creating value for stakeholders are indeed impressive. Many authors have reported on the successful evolution of numerous Silicon Valley firms, but few have sought to systematically understand the lessons that could apply much more broadly—in a variety of industries and firms throughout the world. Dr. Chris Meyer has done just that and done so very successfully.

The core premise of this book is that while downsizing,

restructuring, and reengineering may be essential first steps for many firms, establishing an *attitude* of growth—relentless growth—is what enables an organization and its people to achieve their goals. Furthermore, growing from within through the creation of new products and services is fundamental, because virtually all other growth strategies depend on the capabilities that successful internal growth provides. Without the ability to grow internally, acquisitions stagnate—they can even sink the firm. Growing through new channels, new geographies, and new markets also requires the ability to innovate and manage the creation of new products or services. Rarely can an existing product or service be effectively transplanted without significant change. Thus, a basic tenet of *Relentless Growth* is that if you yourself can't innovate, the chances are slim that growing something that you buy or seek to create through a joint venture or partnership will succeed.

Building on this fundamental notion, Dr. Meyer convincingly demonstrates that innovation demands a different set of management skills and processes than those required for managing an existing set of operations. Innovation creates new knowledge, for example, whereas operations applies existing knowledge and refines it. The innovation process requires a more subtle hand and control mechanism than does operations. When the "operations mindset" is unconsciously applied to the pursuit of innovation, therefore, it chokes and constrains it. Although there are some very operational elements to innovation, this book points out a number of places where those are exactly the wrong things to do rather than the right things to do.

At the heart of this book are five principles that can guide management action and lead to the kind of growth attitude and resulting performance improvements so typical of Silicon Valley firms:

1. Generating and spreading a "positive paranoia" about the need for forward movement and change
2. Getting everyone in the organization looking out (i.e., being externally focused) rather than looking in

3. Flattening the organization and blurring boundaries through the use of open, "high-velocity" information
4. Promoting people with passion and rewarding them with a significant "stake in the game"
5. Going for the gold by repeatedly setting stretch goals, taking action, learning from failure as adeptly as success— and doing it all again.

Using a variety of stories and a conversational tone that captures the color and flavor of Silicon Valley, Meyer shows how these principles have been applied in a variety of Silicon Valley firms and how they can be applied to one's own business. A manager can use these five principles to perform a self-assessment or take a single element and systematically apply it.

This pragmatic and readable book will be especially useful for executives who are responsible for creating successful innovation and growth, yet dependent on the technical development group (for example, marketing, operations, and field service and support). The book can enable those so frequently left out or confused at the front end of the innovation process to participate and contribute more effectively to the overall success and expansion of the business.

In addition, because *Relentless Growth* speaks to new services as well as new products, it can be of great help to firms for which service is becoming increasingly important to their market position and product offerings. Furthermore, while service development has differences and is far less well developed and robust than hardware product development in most organizations, this book illustrates how the same set of principles holds. And, though services are not covered as extensively as the product side, this book goes much further than most regarding innovation in services.

The experience and background of its author contribute to making *Relentless Growth* so effective. Few other writers have had the experience of being an executive in a high-technology setting (Zilog and Silicon Graphics), plus being an executive in a traditional business (Exxon Chemical), plus having the disci-

pline and research training provided by a Ph.D. in applied be-
havioral sciences, organizational strategy, and product/service
development. Add to this Dr. Meyer's extensive consulting
background focused on how to adapt and apply what works in
the Valley to firms like Cummins Engine, Procter & Gamble,
and Emerson Electric, as well as to emerging Silicon Valley
firms—and it's clear that his perspective and knowledge are
unique.

Finally, this book complements and builds on Dr. Meyer's
first book, *Fast Cycle Time* (Free Press, 1993). Rather than cov-
ering the basics of development teams as was done in that
book, for example, *Relentless Growth* looks at what it takes to
keep knowledge workers motivated and how to manage networks of teams. Similarly, the chapter on measurement builds
on the earlier book's description of the "dashboard concept"
and explores why most organizations need to change not only
the measures they employ but the mindset and processes used
to interpret and apply the data those measurement systems
yield. Perhaps most important, in every chapter the author has
very effectively demonstrated how to turn principles and concepts into action.

Professor Steven C. Wheelwright
Class of 1949
Professor of Business Administration
Harvard Business School
Boston, Massachusetts

Preface and Acknowledgments

Ever since I moved here in the early 1980s, life in the Silicon Valley has delighted, fascinated, and occasionally dismayed me. Where else can you find a chain of computer superstores such as Fry's Electronics, which started as a grocery business and continues to sell potato, corn, and silicon chips under the same roof—soft drinks and cappuccino along with PCs, test equipment, and electronic components? In many ways, Fry's is a hologram of Silicon Valley. Walking through one of its stores shortly before Christmas exposes you to the Valley's polyglot culture of Asian immigrants, Hispanic Americans, Stanford professors, venture capitalists, and maybe the next Steve Jobs. They're here because they love buying the latest technology just as much as they do developing it.

While the exciting products and services produced here are why Silicon Valley is known in every corner of the world, its more fundamental contribution is the workstyle and spirit of growth and innovation that started with Hewlett-Packard and grows more robust every day. The old Chinese proverb says that being given a fish lets you eat for a day; learning to fish lets you eat for a lifetime. Constantly learning how to fish *better* is what sets Silicon Valley apart, and the desire to document this drive is why I wrote this book. The Valley leans into the future, turning new ideas into reality with a sense of confidence that is exhilarating—and most importantly, applicable (in whole or part) to any other region, company, or industry in the world.

As an executive, educator, researcher, and consultant, I've had the good fortune to work with and learn from some of the Silicon Valley's best companies and leaders. I've also had a similar opportunity with companies far beyond the Valley, including Procter and Gamble, Ford Motor Company, and Honeywell. While the business pressures within each of these companies and their industries are as different from each other as they are from the Valley's, each has proven that intelligently adapting the Silicon Valley approach to growth and innovation not only works—it often works wonders.

In this learning process, I've benefited from the wisdom and kindness of my clients, colleagues, and friends. Clients provide a living laboratory, albeit with very real business risks that make their contribution even more noteworthy. Therefore I must give a special thanks to Mike Hackworth, Suhas Patil, Bob Dickinson, Bill Chu, Jim Clardy, Satish Gupta, Mike Canning, Kenyon Mei, Tom Kelly, Bill Housley, Mark Wilson, Kaj Linden, Ned Barnholt, Susan Curtis, Tom Vos, Dick Anderson, Duane Hartley, Peter Gaarn, Stu Winby, Bill Kelvie, Donna Callejon, Steve Deggendorf, Frank Marshall, Karen Beumer, Tim Solso, Jack Edwards, Jim Henderson, Roberto Cordero, Joe Loughrey, Donna Van Klompenberg, Mike Brown, Jane Creech, Mark Jackson, Warren Meyer, Chuck Knight, Pat Sly, Paul Gress, Ken Lee, Neil Hagglund, Bob Aron, Bob Boggs, and Linda Bayuk.

My work life is enhanced by my fine colleagues who work beside me at Integral. They test and extend my thinking through their critiques and contributions. The efforts of my Integral colleagues—Jeff Elton, Dan Foster, Peter Hiscocks, Eric Mankin, and Ed Tuttle—are woven into the ideas expressed in this book. The ideas and personal support from Integral founders Steve Wheelwright, Kim Clark, Bruce Stangle, and Mike Koehn have had tremendous value from the day that Steve first suggested I work with Integral.

Though they are not cited by name, I also want to acknowledge the contribution that all of the Integral people have made at one time or another in making this book possible.

As a citizen of the Valley, I prefer to work in partnership, and so I would be remiss without acknowledging those people outside of Integral who have helped me transform experience and practice into this manuscript. First are the executives who shared their time for interviews, such as Wayne Oler, Dave Pottruck, Dave Brown, John Chambers, Ned Barnholt, Ed McCracken, Ron Braniff, Charlie Peters, Steve Berkeley, and Deb and Thanos Triant. There are also those whose work parallels my own and who regularly and generously provide their counsel, including Tony Hope, Ralph Katz, Steve Pile, Geoff Moore, Jonno Hanafin, and Rick Ross.

For me, writing a book begins long before I ever pick up that first sheet of paper; it starts with a vision that is in part stimulated by what others have said and written. In this regard, my thinking has been strongly influenced by the work of Gary Hamel, C. K. Prahalad, Peter Senge, James Brian Quinn, Chris Argyris, Donald Schon, Hau Lee, Kathleen Eisenhardt, Barry Richmond, Marco Iansiti, Clayton Christensen, Gary Pisano, Rebecca Henderson, Kim Clark, Steve Wheelwright, George Fisher, and Jack Welch.

On balance, I've learned that a second book is not any easier to write than the first, though hopefully the results are better. This book would never have come together as it has without the diligence, experience, and wise guidance of my editor, Bob Wallace, combined with the constant encouragement of my literary agent, Jim Levine. Nor would I have ever made it through this second journey without the commitment and friendship of Marci Kahn, who pitched in during a crisis to turn handwritten scribbles into a legible manuscript. Rashell Young also stepped forward when late hours of typing were required.

Each time I start a writing journey, I know it's absurd to expect perfect thinking or phrasing in a first draft. But that doesn't mean I don't act as if this time will be different. Just as Valley workers struggle with the tensions and minor failures inherent in the creative process, often turning themselves into something a little less polite, patient, or available than normal, so do I. My loving wife, Nancy, not only bears the brunt of this but consistently sees through the squall to the sunny shores beyond—and, in doing so, helps me move forward. Like an archaeologist carefully dusting off a new discovery, her caring critiques consistently help me sharpen and separate what's important from the collage of early thoughts and drafts. She is often joined by the three rapidly growing young men in our family in pulling me along, all the while helping me keep this and any work in the broader perspective of life itself.

As you begin this book, I'm reminded of what my former mentor, Herb Shepard, used to say to me at the end of a day's work: "I hope I was helpful to you." In that same spirit, I hope this book helps you and your company grow by making you a better, wiser, and more courageous innovator.

Introduction

You can't shrink your way to greatness.
—Gary Hamel

If a business leader kidnapped by aliens in 1985 had landed back on Earth in the 1990s, he or she might have thought that most executives had taken their firms to some corporate fat farm. Instead of Richard Simmons leading the flabby and overweight as they sweated off the pounds, we had Michael Hammer and his devotees leading re-engineering calisthenics across the globe. The exercise was worthwhile, but enough is enough. It's time to stop pruning and start creating new value for our customers and ourselves.

WELCOME TO SILICON VALLEY

Nowhere is the power and excitement of growth more evident than in Silicon Valley. Relentless growth has transformed these former apricot orchards just south of San Francisco into the home for one-third of the 100 largest technology companies created in the United States since 1965. But although its economy now rivals any in the world, Silicon Valley has also had more than its share of failures. In fact, one of the factors that make the Valley unique is that failure here is understood to be an integral aspect of the growth process. Investors, entrepreneurs, and technologists will readily abandon a company or technology that looks unlikely to thrive, using what they have learned to jump-start the next innovation effort.

Four features distinguish the Silicon Valley's economy from that of other regions. First, growth in the Valley is driven by innovation. Even when acquisitions are involved, the typical goal is to spur innovation by combining complementary technologies and resources. Second, the Valley is the world's oldest, most advanced, and most successful knowledge economy—because knowledge work is the foundation of innovation. Third, the competitive intensity and pace of today's global competition is old news to the Silicon Valley. After it nearly lost the semiconductor industry to Japan in the early 1980s, healthy fear and intense foreign and domestic competition have propelled the Valley to compete in what John Chambers (the CEO of networking king Cisco Systems) describes as "dog years": a year here is worth seven years in other industries. Fourth, despite the headline-grabbing power of the admittedly sexy technology embedded in its products and services, *the Silicon Valley's most important contribution is a combination of a new work spirit* (which I call the Growth Attitude) *and a new approach to innovation.*

While others competed by downsizing, reengineering, and leveraging financial assets, Silicon Valley was creating and delivering new value. The results speak for themselves. In 1990, Silicon Valley electronics exports were greater than $11 billion, almost one-third of the nation's total. Between 1975 and 1990, Silicon Valley firms added 150,000 new technology-related jobs.[2] And if Detroit had followed the same price-performance curve that the Valley has achieved in semiconductors, today's cars would travel at supersonic speed, consume less than one ounce of fuel per 10,000 miles, and cost less than 25 cents to buy.[3]

This book answers two questions: (1) How does Silicon Valley grow successfully through innovation, and (2) how can you adapt this innovation methodology to work in your company? Although the pressures of ever-shorter product life cycles, rapidly changing technology, and cutthroat competition may be more intense in the Valley than in your industry, they are now felt almost everywhere. Think of the Silicon Valley's dog-years pace as an accelerated innovation research laboratory, from which you can take the most relevant learning for use in your company. Furthermore, the Valley's distinctly American flavor means that what works here probably has a better chance of being applicable to your company than the latest technique from Asia.

The assumptions behind this book can be summarized as follows:

1. The searing heat of today's globally competitive environment, combined with rapid changes in technology, can quickly melt winners into losers. Standing still equals falling behind.
2. While innovation isn't the only route to growth, it's essential to creating *sustainable* growth. A new acquisition can quickly turn into a dead weight if you can't innovate.[4] Similarly, expanded distribution channels will level off eventually unless you can generate a continuous stream of new products and/or services.
3. The underlying strategy, leadership, structures, processes, and skills that drive innovation are fundamentally different from those that are used to manage daily business operations. Not only do the traditional skills not work, they'll smother innovation quicker than you can say Dr. Kevorkian.
4. Innovation is not a mysterious black box. It can be learned and managed in both service and product industries.

As a result of these truths, *every* manager needs to learn how to lead, nurture, and manage innovation. In today's world, this often includes managing and developing new technologies. The problem is most of us were never schooled in innovation, or technology management. Even those with technical degrees were taught their respective disciplines, but not how to lead, develop strategy or manage technology-based change. Silicon Valley lives on the leading edge—or, as the locals sometimes call it, the bleeding edge—of this change. My thesis, confirmed by personal experience, is that you can improve innovation dramatically in your company by taking what the Valley has learned and adapting it to your company.

INNOVATION IN SERVICE INDUSTRIES

Most of the innovation literature focuses on product development, saying little about service development even though an overwhelming majority of U.S. workers are employed in the service sector. As those of you who work in the service economy know, many of its competitive requirements and issues are very different from those in the product arena; over the last few years, though, I've had the opportunity to apply the model and tools described in this book to several clients in the service sector. While the field of service innovation is quite new, my hope is that this book can be equally helpful to those of you who work in service industries.

But I'll give you fair warning: There are no silver bullets in here. What happened in Silicon Valley did not occur as a result of any magic formula. In many respects, people simply dropped the old methods and did what made sense.

YESTERDAY'S SOLUTIONS
CREATE TODAY'S OPPORTUNITY

Reengineering was necessary to realign firms to take advantage of the power of information technology. Additionally, many companies had become fat, acted dumb, and were happier than they should have been about their competitive standing. The get-fit regimes, though, caused suffering for the displaced workers—and a proportionally increased workload among those who remained, since the promised benefits of reengineering rarely arrived at the same time that their colleagues departed. More importantly, the downsizing plans failed to recognize that you can't shrink your way to greatness. You can't squeeze costs to make profits from flat revenues forever, nor can you put unimproved products into new geographical markets indefinitely.

It's time, then, to put our trim, in-shape corporate bodies to work on the opportunities before us. There's a new world out there, and it's increasingly hungry and wealthy enough to buy new services and products that add value. It's time to innovate and grow.

1

Knowledge

The Motherlode of Value

Have you ever received one of those birthday cards that plays "Happy Birthday" when you open it? You probably chuckled and then casually threw it away without realizing that you just discarded more computing power than existed in the entire world prior to 1950![1] This seemingly simple product signals what growing through innovation is all about.

For about three dollars (not adjusted for inflation), you get an absolute marvel of innovation. The hardware alone is astounding. The card uses a long-lasting miniature battery that relies on complex chemical reactions to provide power and ensure a long shelf life. A microswitch triggers a computer that's half the size of a postage stamp, programmed with music, and attached to a miniature speaker. All this is secured by a strong, lightweight adhesive to recycled paper stock that might have started its life as the front page of a metropolitan newspaper (and will probably be resurrected to a third life when your trash is picked up later this week). The complete set of knowledge required to create this product did not exist ten years ago, yet this inexpensive product exemplifies how sophisticated even the simplest products have become.

Impressed yet? There's more. What good is this magical birthday card, after all, if you can't put it into your loved one's hand? If you're as forgetful about birthdays as I am, you're going to need what amounts to a personal delivery service—someone who'll come to your office, get the card, and ensure it gets halfway around the world in a single day. As you probably know, Federal Express, UPS, or Airborne Express all provide this "personal" service. In addition, if you want to check where the card is any time after it's picked up, you can call a toll-free number or even access the shipper's computer directly through the Internet. The service is as amazing as the product!

In this new world, the boundaries between products and services fade rapidly. Just as bricks have little value without mortar to hold them together, today's most advanced products are held together by a mortar composed of equally advanced services. The combination transforms stand-alone products like our birthday card into a seamless, value-rich solution.

Before we leave this compelling yet simple example, don't think that our birthday card and delivery service are just for the affluent, or only available in Silicon Valley. You can buy and send this card from anywhere in North or South America, Europe, or Asia. Next year, the same product will undoubtedly cost less, sing longer and louder, and perhaps be able to record your own voice. This is the new world of competition—a fierce contest set in a truly global context, with more capable players, higher stakes, and vastly different rules of engagement from those that we have enjoyed to date.

In this chapter, I'll explain how knowledge has become the dominant component of customer value, and why this makes innovation a critical competitive requirement. As you will see, the new economy is led by those who create, find, and/or combine knowledge into new products, services, and distribution methods faster than their competitors. As their capability to create and combine new knowledge spreads across the globe, it creates new markets. The interaction between these trends sets up a powerful reinforcing cycle.

KNOWLEDGE AS THE SOURCE OF VALUE

It used to be that companies ventured offshore in search of raw materials—or, more frequently, cheap labor. Raw materials (and the energy required to convert them) are less critical due to tremendous progress in process technology. Since the late 1970s, the amount of energy required to produce a given amount of GDP has fallen an average of 2 percent each year![2] Concurrently, the knowledge component of products and services—and the brains required to produce and use them—has increased dramatically in importance. Valley leaders like Sun Microsystems, Hewlett-Packard, and Intel today set a new standard, applying the same fervor to finding *cheap knowledge* that they previously used to search for cheap labor.

In the industrial age, competitive strength was determined by who had access to raw materials, cheap labor, and the capital for conversion. Large machines characterized the thinking, as well as the work itself. Employees were treated as parts (oiled by wages) that could be replaced if they broke. Work processes such as the assembly line were designed to constrain rather than exercise human capabilities; Henry Ford once asked in frustration, "How come when I want a pair of hands, I get a human being as well?"[3] It was this mentality that eventually spawned unions—when you treat people as machines, they eventually reach a point where they fight back. Piece-rate pay schemes fit neatly within the model by providing the faster "machines" with more pay. Machine-age thinking fit a machine-dominated world.

Knowledge work existed back then, too; it was called the boss. A machine needs direction, and that was the boss's job. As products and services became more complex, though, it became impossible for the boss to know every job detail or piece of equipment. For the equipment technology of today's service operations center or manufacturing facility, this complexity is even more overpowering. Nowhere has this been more evident than in Silicon Valley.

Transforming Sand into Knowledge

The historical foundation of the Valley's success is the semi-conductor. On an eight-inch wafer of purified, molten sand are hundreds of chips, each the size of a thumbnail. Etched on each chip are lines and layers of alternating conductive and resistive materials that form complex electric circuits. Line width at the current state of the art is .25 microns, about one-quarter the size of a human hair. With transistor counts skyrocketing into the millions, these devices are just as difficult to design, test, and program as they are to manufacture. Each chip embodies hundreds of person-years of work and aggregated scientific knowledge.

The cost of a new wafer fabrication factory is more than $1 billion, but the raw materials (concrete, steel, plastic, copper, and so on) that make up the building and equipment inside don't add up to anywhere near that much. The high cost reflects the science that's embedded in the equipment. The skills required to run this equipment are equally sophisticated. Contrast the associate degree that the average wafer fabrication technician possesses to the educational level of farmers who moved to Detroit to work on Henry Ford's first assembly line.

All Knowledge Isn't the Same

To understand the impact of knowledge on value definition, creation, and delivery, we first have to expand our understanding of knowledge itself. When most people talk about knowledge, they're usually referring to explicit knowledge[4]— the kind that can be easily written down (for example, a chemical formula or an engineering schematic). Explicit knowledge is what you find in computer data banks, text-books, and academic journals; once created, it is easily captured, distributed, and used by people other than the creator.

While explicit knowledge can create a competitive advantage—as in the case of a patent for a new technology—its half-life is increasingly brief. Once we know something can be done, much less time and money is required to imitate, reverse engineer, or clone it than was needed to demonstrate its initial viability.

For example, after Intel spent $1 billion and more than a year to create its 486 microprocessor, Cyrix was able to produce a clone in approximately 18 months for just $10 million. The same thing happened with Apple's laser and Hewlett-Packard's inkjet printers. These products were the first to reach the market, but Apple quickly found itself facing competition from none other than Hewlett-Packard, while H-P found its business under attack from Canon (who happens to supply the laser print engines for both Apple and HP).

A second type is tacit or implicit knowledge, which you may think of as personal and context-specific "know-how." Tacit knowledge is far less tangible and so deeply embedded into an organization's operating practices that it's often nearly invisible, being described broadly as just "the way we do things around here." For individuals, it's often referred to as experience or intuition; in organizations, we often call it culture. What we refer to as intuition, though, are really bits of knowledge that we've gained and combined with other bits in ways that are not easily traced or described. Tacit knowledge includes relationships, norms, values, and standard operating procedures. Because tacit knowledge is much harder to detail, copy, and distribute, it can be a sustainable source of competitive advantage. While competitors such as Six Flags can experience and study Walt Disney Corporation's legendary service capability at its amusement parks, none have duplicated it.

The Implications of Knowledge as Value

The shift to knowledge—both explicit and tacit—as the primary source of value has five important implications that change what it takes to compete effectively:

1. *The most visible output of knowledge work is explicit knowledge, but the creative process is largely tacit.* Certainly the act of discovery is not a very explicit process. Product innovations such as Post-it™ Notes don't follow a predefined, rational path, although the execution that follows the initial idea does have explicit elements. In contrast, traditional business processes such as assembly lines or accounting departments are highly explicit. Managing innovation—a process with a high tacit knowledge content—using techniques that work well with explicit knowledge is about as effective as dancing by watching your feet instead of feeling the music. I'll examine this point in more detail when I discuss how to manage the innovation process.

2. *Explicit knowledge is increasingly quick and easy to distribute worldwide.* For thousands of years, knowledge could only be passed on by word of mouth; centuries later, it was captured by monks in books. Now, however, it is distributed instantaneously through global electronic networks. (In a recent ad, IBM portrayed monks as technology-savvy Internet surfers!) Today's graduate students in Vienna, New York, or Kuala Lumpur all have equal access to the latest scientific journals.

It therefore might make more sense to sell or license explicit knowledge—for example, through franchising—to an existing local operative rather than establish a business of your own. Why? Because local entities already possess the hard-to-acquire tacit knowledge of regional operating practices, laws, and customs. If you provide the explicit knowledge regarding the base product or service, the local firms can leverage their tacit knowledge to jumpstart your firm into markets across the globe.

This leverage, though, cuts both ways; foreign companies can be just as successful on our shores as we are on theirs. For example, the baby-boom generation that followed World War II is graying in European and Asian populations as well as the United States. The Swedish national telecommunications company is actively marketing systems aimed at the home health care market, and these kinds of products and services will transfer easily to the U.S. markets for our aging population.[5] While still only about a third the size of the fees the United States generates from exporting knowledge, American payments for knowledge imports are growing two and a half times faster than receipts. If these trends continue, America will be a net importer of ideas by the second decade of the twenty-first century.[6]

3. *When it is embedded in products and services, explicit knowledge dramatically lowers the cost of the basic infrastructure required to compete in any industry.* Look at what telecommunications technology and the personal computer have done to the cost of setting up a professional service corporation. With a phone, a fax machine, and a well-equipped PC, an individual attorney can create a professional presence that is indistinguishable from the most prestigious firm on Wall Street.

The expansion and availability of explicit knowledge enables Silicon Graphics and Sun Microsystems to outsource manufacturing to firms like Solectron, a company with no products of its own. The task of stuffing, soldering, testing, and assembling circuit boards requires a great deal of explicit knowledge but very little tacit knowledge. At the same time, Solectron or anyone else would be hard-pressed to design either company's products, for that is highly dependent on each company's tacit design methodologies as well as explicit technical knowledge.

The dramatic increase in embedded explicit knowledge is one reason that the labor force has grown by more than 50 percent from 1970 to 1992, while those employed by Fortune 500 companies decreased 21 percent. The message is clear: As tools and infrastructure costs continue to fall while their power increases, nearly anyone can establish themselves as a viable competitor in any but the most capital-intensive industries. What increasingly differentiates success and failure is how well you locate, leverage, and blend available explicit knowledge with internally generated tacit knowledge. The bottom line is, how well can you innovate?

4. *All knowledge grows through use, while physical assets such as materials are depleted by use.* Using knowledge creates more opportunities, which in turn create more knowledge. This principle has implications for timing your entry into a new market or technology. You have to enter some markets earlier than you would otherwise because it takes time to learn the required knowledge, but your discoveries about what works and what doesn't can define the market to your advantage. For example, Yahoo!—one of the first companies to provide Internet indexing services—built a reputation and market presence that they've been able to defend successfully despite growing competition.

The corollary is that knowledge depreciates through lack of use. If you stop pushing the edge and coast, you very quickly find yourself being passed by. Look what happened to Apple's leadership in the PC computer interface. Although Mac zealots may proclaim that Windows 95 is the equal of the Macintosh in 1989, the Macintosh operating system has not continued to move forward. By resting on its laurels, Apple has seen the difference between the Macintosh and Windows operating systems become virtually nonexistent.

5. *The explosion of knowledge growth, combined with rapid distribution, makes it difficult to sort and stay on top of the available knowledge within your industry.* In the field of cardiovascular science, for example, more than 80,000 articles were published in the last six months of 1992 alone.[7] A global knowledge economy rewards not only the creators of new knowledge but those who can identify and combine knowledge effectively.

AS KNOWLEDGE GROWS, SO DOES THE GLOBAL MARKET

The ability to compete by creating value through knowledge is no longer the exclusive province of traditional economic powers. Today's schoolgirl in Singapore receives as good an education, if not a better one, as her counterpart in Palo Alto,

California. She also prints her school assignments on a DeskJet™ printer from Hewlett-Packard, possibly a later model than her peer in Palo Alto has. Her family's standard of living and discretionary income put her squarely in the middle class. She is well on the way to becoming a valuable future employee and consumer.

Does knowledge creation occur outside traditionally strong economic leaders? Well, if I had asked you in 1991 to name the country that in five years would be home to the world's second-largest manufacturer of cellular phones, would you have answered Finland? (In 1996, Finland's Nokia—formerly known more for its snow tires than for world-class digital technology—gained market share at the expense of world leader Motorola.) Clearly, knowledge creation is happening everywhere.

This spread of knowledge is creating a global middle class of new customers (and competitors) in nearly every corner of the world. Firms that don't recognize this change and stay within their domestic borders, particularly in slower-growing First World nations, will miss out on much more than an additional revenue opportunity. They will develop neither the competencies nor the presence required to participate in the global marketplace. Over time, they will find that unless they are protected by national tariffs, for which the trend is less rather than more, they will also be decreasingly competitive at home.

Traditional early entrants in foreign markets, such as Procter & Gamble or Coca-Cola, provide low-cost basics. But as the global middle class grows, they want to buy more than bare essentials. Today's sophisticated buyers from Beijing to Rio de Janeiro seek the same products and services that are found in the boutiques on Ste. Honoré in Paris, or within the bustling consumer electronics arcades of Tokyo's Akihabara. People with knowledge have a large appetite for such knowledge-rich products.

Once people begin to move beyond essentials, the demand for services grows, as is demonstrated by the growth of U.S.

retailers abroad. Toys 'R' Us is going gangbusters in Japan despite meager 0.5 percent economic growth forecasts. Kmart, while struggling to get back on track in the United States, has a growing operation in the Czech Republic and started operations within Singapore in 1994.[8] Retail champion Wal-Mart is scouting new markets this year after success with Mexican discount stores. Knowledgeable people seek services that support their knowledge.

As the thirst for new products and services grows, tangible and intangible barriers to open competition are challenged.[9] Deregulation and privatization of government has spread far beyond U.S. borders, including even such conservative sectors as banking.

Take the Citicorp example in Asia. Asia's rapid development and economic liberalization opened the door to dramatically expand consumer banking;[10] still, it wasn't easy. Government rules sharply limited the number of branches foreign banks could open, and local cultures frowned on borrowing. Beginning in the 1980s, Citicorp employed heavy lobbying and innovative thinking to get around these limitations. Winning local customers with American-style round-the-clock telephone banking, it also used local messengers to pick up deposits. Then Citibank introduced car loans just as the Japanese were starting to export cheaper cars to countries such as India, Indonesia, the Philippines, and Pakistan, where the banking industry was least developed. Being an innovator enabled the bank to establish margins of 24 to 40 percent annually; while this may sound outrageous, it was the only alternative to local loan sharks who charged 60 to 72 percent. Today Citibank achieves a higher return on assets in its emerging-market business than it does domestically, and emerging-market consumer deposits are nearly as large as their market-leading domestic share.

The shift from a materials-based to a knowledge-based economy also subverts traditional trade barriers. Customs agents can stop physical products at ports of entry or require licensing to provide services, but stopping the flow of innovative ideas is nearly impossible. Compared to the fax machines that circumvented Chinese authorities' ability to censor communications during the tragic uprising in Tiananmen Square, the potential of the Internet is virtually unlimited. In the meantime, while knowledge transfer is currently only a small piece of total international transactions (about 2 percent of total trade), for well over a decade world payments for royalties and licenses have been growing 75 percent faster than world trade, and 50 percent faster than overall output.[11]

Retreating to the protection of national boundaries is not a sustainable solution. Peugeot, Renault, Fiat, and Alfa Romeo have all withdrawn from the United States' import car market where they weren't competitive—but do you think they'll thrive for long by serving only their domestic markets? I seriously doubt it. In a global economy, you can run, but you can't hide. It takes only a quick glance at your favorite sport to understand the positive contribution of competition. When you're exposed to the pressures of competing on today's global playing field, you can't help but lift your level of play.

Not only does the spread of knowledge set off a chain reaction of global market growth, it simultaneously improves global production capabilities, which in turn creates opportunities that we've never seen before. For example, if you combine the new capability of former Third World countries such as Malaysia with those of multinational competitors from traditional economies, you end up with a true round-the-clock economy. In the most profound sense, the sun never sets on leading-edge innovators like Morgan Stanley or Hewlett-Packard. The work rotates with the sun; when the market traders or engineers end their respective workdays in California, Asia clocks in, followed by Europe! Think of it: it's the equivalent of having three shifts, but everyone works days.

THE CASE FOR RELENTLESS GROWTH

Change creates opportunity, but only for those who recognize and seize it. Cisco, Bay Networks, and Cabletron stole the data communication networking business out from under the noses of the phone companies. The large telcos couldn't see the explosive implications of the digital world on data communications through their glazed, regulatory eyes. After living so long in a regulatory stupor, the sense of urgency that permeates the Valley was missing from their experience—so they didn't act. And of those who did act, only Cisco Systems has grown relentlessly enough to dominate the market. The moral: Seeing is the first step, seizing the second, and continuously innovating is the third.

If you choose not to participate, watch out! There are no safe havens. Someone will always be nipping at your heels, trying to attract your customers, suppliers, investors, and employees over to their team. Even in slower-growing economies, innovation redefines growth opportunities. Look at what Roger Penske achieved at Detroit Diesel. Most people would not think of diesel engines as a growth industry; by streamlining operations and introducing electronic fuel injection before his competitors, however, Penske took Detroit's market share from 3 percent to 20 percent over five years.[12] Likewise, Detroit's competitor, Cummins Engine, has established partnerships in Asia and Eastern Europe to bolster growth in the coming decade.

Growth through innovation reinvigorates a company. Look at what Chrysler's series of innovations has achieved. First, the minivan—a Ford concept, but one that Chrysler brought to market first. Then, the Viper—not a financial windfall, but an image vehicle and invigorating. Next came the LH cars, with their cab-forward design. Shortly after that, the Neon—a U.S. compact that is competitive and actually might make money! Then came the pickup truck, with a macho design that mimicked the big eighteen-wheelers. Just this year, Chrysler has introduced another image vehicle—the Prowler, a retro-styled hot rod. And that's just their products.

They've changed their entire design process and constructed a billion-dollar design center to foster rapid innovation. Like a Silicon Valley company, they rely on supplier partnerships for success (more so than either Ford or GM). And the financial results speak for themselves. Today they enjoy the highest profits per vehicle, and also the best morale in the U.S. auto industry. Walking through Chrysler is no different than walking through the halls of Cisco Systems, Hewlett-Packard, or Oracle. The spirit of relentless growth keeps fresh ideas flowing.

THE UNIQUE U.S. ADVANTAGE

Not long ago, American competitiveness was questioned both at home and abroad. During the decade following World War II, we were more competitive only because there wasn't much competition; most other industrial nations were absorbed in postwar reconstruction. But that wasn't true in the 1970s and 1980s, when we rested on our laurels and were throttled—most frequently by the Japanese, and most visibly in automotive and consumer electronics. Being knocked on our economic keester first, however, also meant that we got started fixing the problems first. While it's going to be a dogfight, the United States is better positioned than many of its competitors for success in the twenty-first century. Below are six reasons why.

1. *American companies are regularly exposed to the world's best competition, on our home turf.* Our companies battle head-to-head with the world's best every day. In our increasingly deregulated economy, companies have little protection.[13] The choices are to get tough and innovate, or get beat. For example, local American shopkeepers have to tackle giants like Wal-Mart head on, whereas our Japanese counterparts can hide behind zoning laws that protect the small storekeeper.

2. *The United States knows how to create jobs.* Since the mid-1980s, approximately 2 million factory jobs have vanished each year, yet the net decline in such jobs over a decade was only about 1 million.[14] Through new startups and small businesses, we have redistributed our workforce from dying

industries to thriving ones. In fact, 18 million new U.S. jobs were added during this same period (a growth rate of 20 percent), while the similar-sized European Economic Community has added just 7 million jobs. And not only have we made the shift, we've grown in industries that have a much brighter future.

3. *The United States has the world's largest installed base of (and most advanced) information technology.* Innovation increasingly relies on information technology to access and distribute knowledge. For almost four years, the United States has been spending more on computers and communications equipment than on all other capital equipment combined.[15] For example, the combination of existing telecommunications and cable infrastructure enables high-speed communications (such as video) with only incremental technology development, whereas Europe and Asia lack this infrastructure. For today's retail competitors, electronic point-of-sale systems combined with bar coding enable automatic restocking of inventory. When combined with increasingly common electronic data interchange (EDI) between companies, they take the concept of the virtual company to a new level: the virtual industry. The effect of this invisible cooperation creates a force more powerful than the traditional Japanese *kiretsu*, because it works in real time.

4. *The service sector in the United States is by far the largest, most productive, and most innovative in the world.* In the context of the global knowledge economy, services become more important as wealth rises and integrated solutions become more important. Retail productivity in the United States is twice that of Japan, and our telecommunications industry holds a comparable advantage over Germany's government monopoly.[16] Meanwhile, the U.S. financial services industry dominates the globe.

5. *Embracing change is a U.S. strength.* Speed is critical to winning the innovation race and while the competition is fierce, the United States excels at major paradigm change. For example, Japanese computer and electronics firms have

not been able to unseat American leaders such as Intel, Microsoft, Quantum, Seagate, or Compaq. Where the tectonic plates that support markets and technologies undergo constant shearing and shifting, the United States has enormous advantages. In contrast, where relatively stable technologies make incremental improvements the basis for advantage, we still have a lot of learning to do.

6. *We know how to partner.* The United States is much more willing to grant local managers authority and influence in the running of foreign subsidiaries. Intel and Hewlett-Packard facilities in Asia are led by locals and now design as well as manufacture products. Meanwhile, even at Uniden—where only 277 of 10,000 employees work in Japan—Japanese executives run all foreign subsidiaries, and most key decisions are made at headquarters.[17]

SUMMARY

Leaders who exploit the new environment by seizing opportunities for growth will redefine the industrial landscape for both their personal and our world's betterment. As I've illustrated, growth at home and abroad provides the seeds of new learning that enable you and your firm to win. And for companies in the United States, the opportunities have never been brighter. In the next chapter, I'll look into what it takes to innovate in the world of relentless growth.

2

The Loose-Tight World
of Innovation

Everyone has a favorite innovation story. Some people like products that challenged an industry's fundamental assumptions (such as IBM's eraserlike pointing device, which is rapidly replacing the trackball on portable computers). Others enjoy seeing an established player get surprised by a newcomer, as Microsoft was by Netscape in the early days of the Web browser wars. Then there are those elegantly simple, yet extraordinarily well-executed ideas that aren't brand new but take today's technology and take advantage of it as nobody has—Merrill Lynch's cash management accounts, for example, or the original Lexus LS400. Or maybe it's something that seems obvious, yet no one ever thought about it before. Point-Cast, a small Silicon Valley company, came up with such a coup when it transformed a common computer product (the screen saver) into a free, personalized up-to-the-minute news service.

The stories we think of tend to have three common elements. First, they are almost always about wildly successful "killer" products or services. Rarely does someone raise an innovation failure, such as the Edsel. Second, without guidance, most people focus on the innovation itself rather than the process that created it. This instinct suggests that all innovation requires is creative people with good ideas. Third, when we do talk about the innovation process, the concept discovery receives the majority of our attention. It's more enthralling to hear about how the idea for 1-800-Flowers came about than it is to discuss the implementation details of flower cutting, storage, and delivery.

As a result, our understanding of what innovation is and what's required to be successful is spotty. With rare exception, most people have a much better grasp of what it takes to run today's business. This may explain why so many find managing innovation to be extremely frustrating. It often seems as though there are only three things that you can count on for certain: whatever is being attempted will take longer, cost more, and not perform as well as you initially thought or were promised. Innovation takes on the aura of a black box—when it's not working, the only thing that you can do is pound on the box (and the people in it).

But innovation does not have to be that mysterious. In this chapter I'll introduce the Innovation System, a model that synthesizes and defines the core elements of innovation. Think of this chapter as an innovation primer, because it establishes the framework that we'll use to reveal the unique innovation practices of Silicon Valley. In addition to describing the model, I'll show you why you must apply it and manage innovation much differently than you would operations. You'll also see that innovation involves hard work, in addition to creativity. In subsequent chapters, we'll drill down, one element at a time, to show you what it is that makes innovation in the Valley so successful and unique.

THE INNOVATION SYSTEM

Five interdependent elements compose the core of the Innovation System (see Figure 2–1). How each element behaves

FIGURE 2–1

The Innovation System

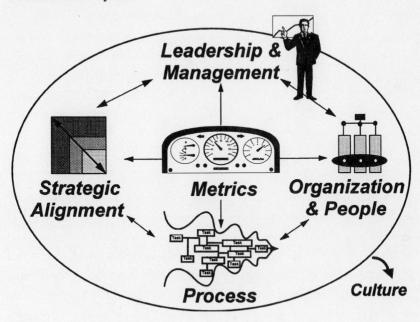

and interacts with the others is determined by the sixth—
your firm's culture, which you may only know as "the way we
work around here." For now, I'll briefly describe each element; in subsequent chapters, I'll detail each one and provide
tools for putting the model to use in your firm.

Leadership and Management

The old saw says that leadership is doing the right thing; management is doing things right. The boundary between the two
is not as crisp as the slogan would suggest, however, and both
are required for effective innovation. Leadership provides inspiration and makes key choices, such as what projects to pursue and when to be "loose" versus "tight." Management skills
are required for the endless details and complex interactions
that are routinely part of any development.

Relative to the other elements in the Innovation System,

FIGURE 2–2

The Actual Route of Profitable Innovation

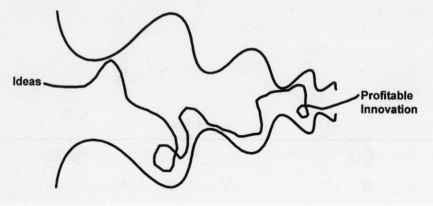

leadership and management are rarely practiced as an independent element. Strategic alignment doesn't occur without leadership, just as the best-designed development process is worthless without strong leadership and ongoing management, and so on. Be careful, though, not to confuse leadership and management with position. This is particularly true in the Valley, where organizations are relatively flat and new ideas and initiatives can start almost anywhere. Leadership and management are just as essential at the front lines of projects and workgroups as they are in the executive suite.

Leading innovation is a delicate process. You need to access all the knowledge you have, but if you don't maintain enough distance from that same knowledge, you won't create anything new. You need to encourage expansive thinking to generate new ideas, but also sift through these ideas to decide which to commercialize. Taking yourself and others into the unknown—and then back again—requires a "loose-tight" style of leadership, as illustrated in Figure 2–2.

Loose-tight leadership alternates the creation of space for idea generation and free exploration with a deliberate tightening that selects and tests specific ideas for further investment and development. While it is necessary throughout the process, looseness dominates the early stages; in the later stages, tightening becomes more important. A Silicon Valley design leader I know describes the innovation process as gradually moving from a gaseous to a solid state.

Modulation is essential to loose-tight leadership; staying in either modality for too long creates serious problems. Those who remain loose generate plenty of ideas, but have difficulty commercializing them. The pragmatics of cost estimation, market testing, operations planning, along with the mundane realities of documentation and pricing, either aren't done well or don't get done at all. For example, Xerox's Palo Alto Research Center has been the creator of such major innovations in computing as the graphical interface and the mouse, yet it did not bring either concept to market.

Those who lock into the tight mode mimic the operations of others and choke off all but the most obvious ideas, subjecting them to the rigors of commercialization far too early. Holding too tight a grip confines innovation to incremental line extensions of existing products that add little value. If a competitor introduces a substantially new alternative, the firm's chances of being knocked out of the ring are quite high.

This is exactly what Visioneer did to Logitech in the PC scanner business. Prior to Visioneer's arrival, your choices in scanner technology were either large, expensive flatbed scanners (which were essentially electronic copiers) or small hand-held devices; Logitech was the leading supplier of hand-held scanners. Hand-held scanners were dependent on the steadiness of your hand; in addition, they had to make two passes to scan any normal sheet of paper. In 1994 Visioneer introduced a new scanner, approximately the size of a box of aluminum foil, that fit between the keyboard and monitor. Using two rollers like an old wringer washer, it handled regular paper, ensured stability, and cost significantly less than a flatbed scanner. Today the Visioneer scanner is built into selected Hewlett-Packard and Compaq keyboards, and the company has a market capitalization of $115 million.

Strategic Alignment

Have you ever driven a car when the front end is badly out of alignment? If so, you know how hard you have to fight to keep the car going straight as one wheel fights to pull it to the left, while the other fights to pull it to the right. Driving is not only unsafe but nerve-wracking, particularly if you have to change direction or stop quickly.

The same is true for a poorly aligned innovation strategy—only it has many more wheels. Business strategy should drive innovation strategy and choices. This sounds so obvious! But if you were to sit down with any executive and discuss the importance of linking innovation strategy to the business strategy, they would say, "Right, of course that makes perfect sense." Frequently, this is not what happens. Instead, at some level that's divorced from the overall corporate strategy, a decision is made to develop a new product or service—and then six months to a year later, people see the problem and say, "Wait a minute, what are we getting into here?"

The cost and time required to create a new product or service are so large that anything less than a perfectly aligned and executed strategy can be extremely wasteful. For example, in 1990 it took twelve years and $231 million to develop a new pharmaceutical.[1] In 1995, the average investment had grown to fifteen years and $400 million,[2] and that doesn't account for risk. (A common rule of thumb in consumer products is that only one in ten is successful.) The basic reality that governs innovation is overpowering: You can pursue anything you want, but you can't afford to pursue everything you want.

You must create an innovation strategy that is aligned with not only your firm's core mission and values but with your future technology, supplier, and manufacturing strategies. Lack of alignment between product and process architectures rapidly increases cost and risk. If your development process and organization structure are not matched to each other and your firm's strategy, you're in even deeper trouble.

That's where strategic alignment comes in. Strategic alignment is the process of linking innovation strategy with corporate goals, strategy, and objectives. It creates a directional beacon that defines which domains to explore and which ones to avoid. Without it, innovation activities drift in the same weightless state that astronauts do—and at potentially the same cost.

In the Silicon Valley, strategic alignment results as much from tacit understandings as explicit ones. And Valley leaders know that you'll never achieve perfect alignment without squelching creativity and experimentation. Organizational norms and entrepreneurial experience continually reinforce the opportunism from which new discoveries and alignment can spring. This is a far cry from many traditional organizations, wherein senior managers can produce paper documents "proving" that all these issues have been thoroughly discussed, resolved, and clearly communicated—yet when you assess the state of innovation in these companies, the working people paint a very cloudy picture. The litmus test for strategic alignment is behavior.

In an aligned organization, innovation decisions and actions reinforce each other; people communicate their intentions and test for congruence; and, most importantly, management's time horizon is always a couple of steps ahead of today's operating issues. Another symptom of alignment is that decisions tend to stick; in an unaligned organization, each subgroup tests every decision from its parochial perspective and jockeys for local advantage.

Process

The innovation process defines who does what, when it should occur, and how to do it. Documented innovation processes tend to be the norm in manufacturing companies. Although most service companies do not have a defined process, typically there is a pattern of practice. In either case, the most common development paradigm is a *phase-gate approach* that breaks the process into a set of phases following the initial idea or concept, each with a gate that must be cleared.

You can think of development as a learning process. The better the process fits the challenges of the business, market, and technology, the more effective your innovation efforts will be. So what are the elements of fit? For starters, does the process ensure that the product or service developed is compelling to customers? Does it guarantee that quality is designed into the product rather than added on later through expensive rework? Does the process ensure timely involvement of the right stakeholders, either inside or outside of the firm? Is the process tuned to take advantage of the latest technologies? Is it fast enough to keep a step ahead of the competition?

Without question, success stories such as the Post-it™ Note underscore the importance that creative insight and spontaneity play in innovation. At the same time, there's no way that I know of to plan *invention*. In fact, the importance of invention can be overstated, since the vast majority of new products and services are neither inventions nor highly dependent on them.[3] What have the Japanese invented to dominate the consumer electronics business? Videotape and compact disc technology were invented by Ampex and Phillips, respectively. Sony, Panasonic, and others repackaged, refined, and integrated the core technology with miniaturization, in product and process.

As you will see, a key reason the Silicon Valley leads the world in innovation is that it's continually reinventing its own innovation process. The traditional phase-gate paradigm is being battered by new approaches, mostly from the software industry. Valley companies also use the technology created here—such as corporate intranets, which I'll discuss later—to dramatically reshape their innovation methods.

Over the last ten years, I have helped conduct hundreds of what I call innovation post-mortems, both in and out of the Valley. In each, my colleagues and I examine a recently completed development, looking for ways to decrease the time required while increasing the quality and performance of the product or service created. I'll detail these findings in a subsequent chapter. For now, let me offer a few top-level generalizations.

First, most documented innovation processes start too late and end too early. They do not adequately link the innovation process with the planning process that creates strategic alignment, nor do they ensure that market penetration and customer acceptance occur after launch. By starting too late, they also fail to provide a clear distinction and transition path between research and development. By ending too early, customer and distribution channel feedback are not incorporated into the next generation of products and services.

Second, they tend to focus on the tasks and timing of a few core disciplines, such as engineering in manufacturing companies, or systems development in service companies. For example, many firms underspecify marketing's role as well as that of support functions such as testing, packaging, etc. Innovation is an insidiously pervasive process that touches nearly everyone in the value chain, both within and outside the firm. This is particularly true as customers increasingly seek complete solutions rather than discrete products and services. Innovation requires a multifunctional process with clear roles and accountabilities.

Third, the tasks and timing are treated as if they are independent of resourcing requirements, task complexity, or scope. The idea seems to be that one development process fits all, be it a brand-new platform or a simple line extension. In part, this is why there has been so little transfer between product and service development. For most service projects, traditional product development processes are overkill.

The importance of process was pounded into many of us by the work of the late Edward Deming, the father of America's quality movement. If you want to change your results substantially, you must change your process substantially. The operating definition of a doomed innovation manager is anyone who consistently uses the same process while expecting a fundamentally different result.

Organization and People

There are three critical factors to this element. First, people are the most essential ingredient in any innovation. Machines, systems, and infrastructure are great for service delivery or manufacturing, but only people can be creative. If you doubt this, ask yourself which would be an easier machine to design: one that makes Velcro™ hooks and fuzzy strips, or one that could invent Velcro™ itself (based on fastening history, customer requirements, and whatever else you'd like to throw in).

Second, organization is more than just boxes on a chart—it channels energy, defines explicit and implicit operating norms, and provides infrastructure. Just as roads and traffic laws govern how cars flow through a town, organization governs how resources flow through a company. If you want to have energy and resources flow into innovation, this is done most effectively by intentional design. Some innovation flows (such as rapid response services) are designed like superhighways, with special vehicles, extra capacity, and limited access to ensure speed. Others (such as safety and regulatory compliance) are like narrow city streets, with multiple intersections to ensure thoroughness.

Third, there is no such thing as a perfect organization, for innovation or anything else. Any organization design makes some things easy to do and other things harder to accomplish. A market-focused business unit helps innovation stay focused on a specific customer segment, but it hinders technical learning across segments; a functional organization does the reverse. In both cases, innovation swims against the current of daily operations. To improve innovation, firms are increasingly using multifunctional project teams that come together for the duration of the project. I'll discuss these alternatives in detail later.

Metrics

Imagine yourself in Chicago's O'Hare Airport at five o'clock in the afternoon on the Friday before Christmas. You and about ten other people are standing next to the ticket counter, hoping to snag one of the remaining first-class upgrades. Just as you're about to repeat your mantra and rub your worry beads for the fifth time—invoking any and all spiritual powers is essential—your name is called. As you board the plane, silently reaffirming your belief in a supreme being, you glance into the cockpit and notice that there is no instrument panel in front of the pilot. You poke your head in, and the pilot says, "Don't worry, we know where we're going." (All of a sudden that upgrade doesn't seem like such a good deal, does it?)

Measures provide the guidance and control system for innovation. Without them, you're flying an expensive, risk-prone craft by the seat of your pants. Like the pilot's instrument panel, a good measurement system presents a balanced view of your situation. It tells you where you are, where you're going, and forewarns you of serious problems.

This last point raises another question: If you could choose between instruments that would tell you only what *will* happen versus what *has* happened, which would you pick? Obviously both have value, yet most development measures tell you solely what has happened. In practice, the five measures that nearly everyone tracks in development are schedule, development cost, product/service cost, quality, and performance; each of these are results measures.

But what if you could tell when you were going off course *before* you drifted too far? For example, schedule slips are commonly caused by inadequate resources, which are usually due to the lateness of the preceding project. Wouldn't tracking resources on hand versus those required provide a predictive schedule indicator? If the systems architect you need to start programming a new insurance policy will be tied up on a current assignment for three more months, it doesn't take a nuclear physicist to figure out your project will be delayed.

PUTTING THE ELEMENTS TOGETHER

The arrows between each of the elements in the Innovation System are essential and reflect the high degree of interdependence among the elements. Without leadership and management, the best process framework can quickly deteriorate into a bureaucratic regime that stifles anyone who tries to use it. Similarly, even highly creative and capable people in a well-designed structure with an effective process framework won't overcome a poorly conceived and misaligned innovation strategy. And if you have every element roaring at high speed but your metrics are inaccurate or inadequate, you won't know whether you're cruising or crashing. In sum, effective innovation results when the five elements work in concert. Let's look at how implementing this innovation model requires a different approach than you would use for most operating processes.

Operating Versus Innovating

Think about your average day. When you arrive at work, you probably don't know what fire you'll be fighting first—but it's also likely that when you find it, it'll look familiar. The tools and resources you'll use to attack the problem will also be familiar. Maybe it's as simple as running out of supplies; you probably know (or can quickly find out) who your supplier is, give them a call, and order replacements. Instances such as this challenge your ability to execute, yet the challenge usually is met by juggling and matching known entities, quantities, and capabilities in the right proportions.

That's the world of daily operations: we know what the results should look like, what steps are necessary to achieve them, and who does what along the way. If we should stray off course, we'll also recognize that. These and other characteristics of daily revenue production are listed in the left-hand column in Figure 2–3. The right-hand side of the Figure scopes the innovation terrain. Innovation has not only multiple routes to whatever goal you choose, but multiple goals as well.

For example, in the world of computer networking, conventional wisdom in 1992 argued that Ethernet was finished; if you didn't get on the new ATM protocol train, you'd be left

FIGURE 2–3

Operating Versus Innovating

Operating: Creating Today's Revenue	Innovating: Creating Tomorrow's Revenue
Steps are pre-defined	Steps are undefined
Steps are mostly sequential	Steps frequently non-linear
Functionally focused	Cross-functional work teams
Redoing work costs money	Reworking is part of learning
One right way and result	Several right ways and results
Clear, shared goals	Unclear, conflicting goals
Facts are clear	Facts are fuzzy
Easy to measure	Tough to measure
Rich historical data	Poor historical data
Forecasting helpful	Forecasting difficult
Short cycle time	Long cycle time
Many common causes	Many special causes
Traditional players/roles	Involves new players/roles

stranded at the station. Five years later, the minority of firms (like Grand Junction, now part of Cisco Systems) that bet on the enhanced product known as Fast Ethernet looked pretty smart, while the ATM world was still struggling. In contrast to operations, where the goals are well-defined and measurable, the first challenge of innovation is deciding where you're going.

Next, of the many paths that might lead to your goal, you have to decide which is the right one to take. When innovating, though, you'll always have less information available to make that choice than you'd like. If you ask your customers, you'll find some aspects that are important to all, as well as many where no one agrees. Technologists will often gravitate to the approach that minimizes the unknowns, although doing so frequently conflicts with the performance improvement your customers want. Operations, marketing, sales, and manufacturing will each have their preferences, in the end confirming that there is no such thing as a perfect path. Plus, you can rest assured that whatever path you ultimately choose will not be exactly the one you travel. Some paths lead to cliffs and chasms that are too high and deep to cross within the time and resource constraints. Successful innovators get used to moving forward, backing up, going sidewise, chasing parallel paths for awhile, consolidating, and then going forward again.

Over the last decade, management trends and fads have made the operations mindset even more dominant. The reengineering phenomenon, which focused its attention on operations, enhanced everyone's skills at diagnosing and improving these processes. Since people were drawn to those things that they do well (and rewarded for doing them), they naturally looked for more opportunities to put these new skills into practice. This has increased the attention most firms pay to operations that generate today's value rather than tomorrow's opportunities.

When you contrast the two lists, it's clear that operations are much less ambiguous than innovation. This might suggest that the primary difference between operations and innovation is the amount of risk. While this is true, once it is defined, you *can* manage and confine risk. Valley venture capitalists do this every day when they invest in new companies. When they put a million dollars of seed capital into a startup, they've limited their risk to a million dollars. The more important differentiation between operations and innovation is *uncertainty*.[4]

Uncertainty is knowing that something will happen, but not much more. For example, the chances of a major earthquake hitting San Francisco within the next fifty years are high, but no one knows when it will strike, how big it will be, and where the epicenter will be.[5] Similarly, the chances that hand-held wireless computers will be hugely successful is high, but when they'll arrive, what they'll look like or be used for, and who will use them is unknown. Uncertainty eludes planning, prediction, and containment. That's why the operations mindset, which likes to define precisely and control key parameters, falls on its face when applied to innovation. You don't know for sure what all the parameters are; frequently you don't know which ones are most important. That's why the "go for it, learn, and correct" innovation strategy of Silicon Valley has been so successful. Don't try to figure it all out ahead of time, because you can't; just take your best shot and adjust as you go.

The implications of this difference are significant. If you try to manage the uncertainty inherent in innovation with tools and thinking designed for the relative certainty of operations, you'll run into trouble. Since operations thinking works best with known outcomes, paths, and variables, you'll have to pretend that many uncertain variables are known, or simply wait until they really are. If you overestimate your knowledge, your plans—while looking crisp on the surface—will be grounded in a quicksand of your own making. You'll be continuously surprised as your assumptions prove false. Since most people don't like surprises, you're quite likely to become more conservative with each one, until there's very little innovation left in your innovation strategy.

If you wait until most of the variables have been determined, though, you won't get involved until it is too late. This frequently happens. Senior management often doesn't know how to contribute in what Don Reinertson calls the "fuzzy front end."[6] When the first sample is ready to go out to customers, they're like bees on honey, because now they can touch it, see it, and feel it. Unfortunately, the leverage and place for their involvement resides in the front of the process, where the initial choices of features, markets, and costs are determined.

The more effective way to deal with uncertainty is to have a process that systematically confronts the unknown with new hypotheses, tests them, and eventually creates new knowledge—in short, a learning process. Therein lies the essence of the difference between innovation and operations. *Innovation is a learning process, the product of which is new knowledge. Operations is a production process driven by existing knowledge.* Additionally, innovators have to select the problems that they'll attack from an infinite number of choices; in operations, most of the problems are known. When the problem encountered cannot be addressed by the existing knowledge, of course, operations must employ the tools of innovation. There are also times when innovation uses the tools of operations.

Innovation Requires Creativity *and* Hard Work

Creativity is the very essence of the human spirit and the source of much of our power. Just when it seems we've painted ourselves into a corner, someone finds a new way out, or maybe makes the corner disappear. People can create newness of such proportion that it redefines our world, as in the case of such product inventions as the car, the personal computer, and the telephone. Similarly, the services made possible by these inventions have become part of our lives. Take away the telephone, and you eliminate takeout food and the mail order industry. The Internet depends on a complex fabric of products (such as modems, computers, and software) combined with services (such as telecommunications, banking, and information).

We can't set a date for inspiration or invention, but we do know quite a bit about the conditions that stimulate both. Although I cannot do justice to the subject of creativity in the limited space available here, the following four factors are actively in play within companies throughout Silicon Valley.

1. *Encouragement.* Creating something new takes hard work. Though it may not look like work if you're not moving papers, putting parts together, or meeting with customers, it's much tougher to create something from a blank sheet than it is to execute an established procedure. Add in the ease with which most of us can generate a maelstrom of self-criticism around any new idea, and you can quickly see the importance of encouragement.

2. *Relevant knowledge and experience.* Without a solid grounding in your field, you'll waste time reinventing the wheel. Used well, a good background helps define the questions that push the frontier.

3. *Compatible difference.* Contact with people who are different from those you normally encounter—but not so different that you can't relate to them—breaks established patterns of seeing and thinking. This contact can be achieved by working on a multifunctional team or visiting a company engaged in similar work but in a different geographical area or industry.

4. *Open space for new ideas.* When the mental or physical surroundings are completely full and familiar, there's no room for anything new. In practice, this "room" can be as simple as quiet time to think. When people are very busy, the chances of something new emerging is quite low. Similarly if you're in a familiar physical setting (such as your office), your thinking will likely follow the patterns of thought that are associated with that setting. Open space provides room to experiment and allows seemingly absurd, nonlinear associations to emerge. Non-linear thinking needs space and stimulation.

The Silicon Valley Workstyle

Silicon Valley companies don't address the factors listed above through disciplined discussion and formal programs. The common approach is a pragmatic openness that invites ideas from anywhere, combined with an absence of firmly set beliefs about what work is supposed to be. Encouragement, for instance, happens along several dimensions in the Valley. Many companies have monthly "all-hands" employee meetings where good ideas are publicly recognized and rewarded. Management by walking around lets senior management hunt for and enjoy chatting with the creative thinkers in the guts of the organization.

In an environment of few rules, leaders also are very responsive to requests and suggestions that will improve results. For example, I recently arranged a benchmarking trip to the Valley for several executives (including the president) of a $6 billion manufacturing company in the Midwest. On the way to a presentation, after joking about the several mobile espresso bars we had passed, the president noticed a fellow carrying what looked like a folded table. Asked about it, the man explained with a cheery smile that it was a massage table. He'd be working in a room upstairs; in fact, he had some openings that afternoon if the president wanted to stop by. Suddenly the espresso bars seemed normal!

On the plane back, the executives' conversation shifted from laughter to serious questioning of the practice. They quickly acknowledged how innovative, nimble, and effective the company was compared to their own. Yet the image of the masseur and his table stuck in their craw. After some discussion, they agreed that although it didn't get in the way of work and might even help, it just didn't *seem* right or appropriate. This last point is what makes the Valley special—what's right and appropriate has been dramatically redefined. Do massage tables and expresso actually, drive innovation? I don't know, but *if* it could help you beat your competitor, wouldn't it make sense to consider it?

Valley companies are also not monolithic. Some companies such as Silicon Graphics grant employees two-month sabbaticals every four to six years. They strongly encourage people not just to relax at home but to engage in some adventure that will refresh their spirits, souls, and thought patterns. Most firms don't have sabbaticals, but they are flexible about granting leaves.

Similarly, these companies create open space and safety for new ideas informally, relying on unconstrained common sense rather than formal committees or programs. Most work hard to minimize the number of rules and regulations they establish, preferring to manage by exception using clearly stated values and rigorous employee-selection processes. Second, as best demonstrated by one of the oldest firms, Hewlett-Packard, there are fewer physical walls in the Silicon Valley than in any other geographic area I know. Cubicles or open spaces dominate. Third, there are no fixed hours or work locations. People might work at home for part of the day, come to a meeting at a business location other than their own, and then "hotel" in an empty office there until they leave. Fourth, the decor both reflects the creativity present and inspires more. Silicon Graphics' buildings use bright colors and inventive design inside and out. Electronics Arts has hallways and cubes covered with toys, posters, and other artifacts that reflect the youthful nature of the video game business. Fifth, several Valley companies have ground rules that limit criticism in the very early phase of ideas. Some go so far during early concept reviews as to require people to offer an alternative rather than just criticize. The goal is to recognize that ideas are just ideas; it's only after we apply them that we can determine if they're good or stupid.

At the same time, Silicon Valley companies don't coddle ideas indefinitely; eventually, you must subject them to others' scrutiny. Until you go public with an idea, it can't be part of life, commercial or otherwise. Going public tests and improves ideas as others play with them. It's like launching a product into the market—until others react, you really don't know the full potential of what you've got.

Although the fundamental purpose of innovation is learning, much of the actual work is mundane. Experiments have to be designed and run, statistics tracked and calculated, reports written and budget codes assigned. Field tests and customer trials, while providing useful information, have an element of repetition as well. There are, if you will, operational elements to innovation, just as there are to running the business. Most experienced developers would agree that even the most dramatic and successful innovation is 10 percent inspiration and 90 percent perspiration.

In the innovation space, the routine tasks have little value by themselves; their purpose is to support the knowledge discovery processes. As I will explore later, firms often shoot themselves in the foot by underinvesting in support resources such as test engineers, thereby creating their own bottlenecks. If development becomes stalled because it takes two weeks to get a test scheduled and run, hiring more designers won't help.

What makes innovation unique as a business process is that creativity and routine are intertwined throughout the process. The focus on each component varies in that creativity often is a more important issue toward the beginning, whereas routine elements dominate the end. To be sure, both components exist throughout. Testing a new idea (such as a drug molecule or a new telephone service) is a relatively routine process that might happen fairly early. Similarly, although packaging or promoting a new product or service requires creativity, it may not take place until later in the innovation process.

SUMMARY

The power of any good model is that it makes it easier to understand complex issues and dynamics. The Innovation System, for example, enables us to separate the elements of innovation so that we can examine them (and their connections to each other) in greater depth. In each subsequent chapter, as I detail the elements of this system, a recurring theme will be the role leaders play within the element under discussion. Let's turn now to see how leaders in Silicon Valley use what I call the Growth Attitude as both the energizer and glue for relentless innovation.

3

Leading ... With an Attitude

Deb Triant, CEO of Checkpoint Software (the premier Internet firewall company), suggests that the challenge of relentless growth is not unlike the one faced by movie stunt actors. Clearly, driving cars into barriers, leaping off tall buildings, or dashing through explosions and flames is fraught with risk and uncertainty. To be successful—especially more than once!—these actors have to manage the risks and cope with the uncertainties. While their goal is to do what looks perilous on film as safely as possible, they know that they'll never eliminate all danger. You do as much as you can, and then you go for it.

The opportunity for disaster exists in business as well. If you charge blindly into situations, your chances of crashing and burning are just as high as they are for the aggressive but inexperienced stunt actor. At the same time, if you try to eliminate all uncertainty and control every risk, you'll find yourself frozen in place, never doing anything new.

You can't reduce this approach to a procedure or a doctrine. It's a predisposition that I refer to as the Growth Attitude: a combination of skill, experience, and judgment, with a dash of courage and often a dose of arrogance. This is a different approach to leading than you'd use in the world of daily operations. In addition, though, today's leaders need a model that addresses the realities of the global economic environment: How do you lead innovation within a globally distributed workforce of knowledge workers? That's the focus of this chapter.

I'll begin in Silicon Valley to show how leaders there inject the Growth Attitude into their firms. This attitude establishes a context within which these executives lead by setting direction, creating strategy, securing resources, defining organization architecture, and ensuring that learning occurs. I'll highlight the unique twists Valley leaders bring to each of these traditional roles, then conclude by showing how the leaders of a more traditional company, Emerson Electric, adopted Valley innovation leadership practices to initiate a drive for growth.

VALLEY ECONOMICS: MARGINS KEEP FALLING AND TIME KEEPS SLIPPING... INTO THE FUTURE

If you spend any time within Silicon Valley, you'll quickly notice a different tone and attitude about growth than you'd find elsewhere. Part of it is a texture and pace to conversations that shows up in meetings and hallway conversations. Another element is the willingness to make a decision a click or two quicker than you might expect it. What stands out is a "go for it" orientation that's buttressed by confidence—and a healthy dose of fear that if you don't get going now, the chances of being passed by someone else are very real. This attitude reflects the economic realities of life in Silicon Valley.

Valley product life cycles are as short as six months in length. This means that if you don't introduce new products with rhythmic regularity, you sit on the sidelines with nothing to sell. (Now you know why high-tech stock charts can look like roller coasters at the state fair.) While every industry has its own market windows, none are as demanding as those in the Valley. First, when the window will open is not always predictable; someone who brings substantial additional value to the market can open a seemingly closed window. Second, if you don't have something new to put into the market when the window opens, don't bother—you can't carry over last year's line like you might with Barbie dolls. Third, even if you hit the window you've got to have the production or operational capacity to deliver what the customer orders wherever and whenever they want it. If you have a production glitch, you can quickly fall out of the window you just hit.

To make matters worse, prices in the high-tech world decline from the moment a product is introduced until it reaches the end of its life. These declines can be as drastic as 25 percent in a quarter (and more normally, that amount per year). The common joke about profit margins in the Valley is that it's like running up a down escalator. Hitting the window gets you back to the top of the down escalator, where you can make serious money; if you're late, though, you fight with the other laggards for the low-margin scraps. This environment literally demands innovation. Without it, you don't grow—and in the Valley, if you don't grow, you die. Relentless growth is a requirement, not a choice.

Valley leaders constantly lean into the future. Today's revenue and any projects past the halfway point are "in the chute"—there's little you can realistically do to change them. When you're riding a down escalator, the present is a ticking time bomb. What counts is the future, which is your only chance of survival. Is it any wonder that a unique attitude develops? Of course, the success the Valley has achieved helps: what started as a coping mechanism has matured into a standard (and successful) operating procedure.

Because most other industries operate under less extreme conditions, they treat time differently. Several current General Motors products use engines and other components that were designed at least ten years ago. Unlike the Valley, the automotive industry doesn't have market windows that slam shut; if you don't have a new product for the next model year, you can carry over last year's model. Need a little breathing room? Do what Detroit calls a face-lift, changing minor components like the dashboard and the grille. Even if you lose some market share, you could gain it back by dropping prices, as GM did to stretch the Chevy Cavalier's life (and it made money doing so).

For GM and others, the future is still an opportunity, but it's also a potentially larger risk than leveraging the present or past and certainly harder to define. A new car program costs a lot of money, and who is to say if it will be successful? Besides, we know much more about past and present technologies and models. This history lends itself to the detail and precision of business operations planning and thinking. In this environment, it's easy to see why it's tough to get leaders to commit to innovation and growth.

Milking the past seems safer and much more defined than creating the future. But is it really? Extending models like the Cavalier helped GM's short-term profits, but in the face of exciting new products from Chrysler and Ford, they dropped further behind their domestic competitors in market share. In contrast, because GM's European operations developed new models while Ford waited too long to update its Sierra and Scorpio models, GM gained market share and enjoyed record profits in Europe.

LEADERS INFECT THEIR FIRMS WITH THE GROWTH ATTITUDE

Steve Berkeley, chairman of disk-drive giant Quantum Corporation, says that leaders who lack the Growth Attitude drive their companies while constantly watching the rearview mirror for *anything* that might fall off; if things get shaky, they hit the brakes. Leaders with the Growth Attitude drive their firm as fast they can, regularly stealing glances in the mirror—but only to check the three or four items they can't afford to lose. If these are threatened, they'll slow down right away; if anything else is wobbling, they'll keep going. As Berkeley states, too many companies are consumed with what they have done and where they've been. In contrast, Silicon Valley companies are excited about what they haven't done and where they haven't been. Valley leaders view the future positively, and they have confidence in their ability to get there. Non-Valley leaders often view the future with apprehension and worry about their ability to execute.

Is the Growth Attitude of value outside Silicon Valley? Absolutely! In fact, it's essential in order to overcome the stagnation of operations and the complacency that naturally occurs as firms age. The far more critical question is, how do you, as a leader, spread the Growth Attitude throughout your firm? There's no question that the attitude starts at the top and works its way down the organization. Let's look at five practices that nationally recognized Silicon Valley leaders employ to spread this attitude.

1. Generate and Spread Positive Paranoia

Leaders with the Growth Attitude have a never-ending paranoia about their competition that gurgles impatiently like an upset stomach. As Dave Pottruck, the president of Charles R. Schwab, described it to me, "Employees are always asking me when is it going to let up? Never. There's no destination that we're going to get to. Thinking that someday we're going to arrive on some pinnacle just isn't going to happen. You've got to enjoy the journey."[1]

Perhaps the most broadly acknowledged paranoid company in the Valley is Intel, whose CEO, Andy Grove, recently wrote a book entitled *Only the Paranoid Survive*. Chief Operating Officer Craig Barrett sharpens this by declaring, "We're competitive paranoids." Does this make sense? Intel is the world's most profitable company, with a near monopoly in the PC microprocessor market. Not only do they have a rich customer base that's locked into their proprietary product architecture, but the cost of building a contemporary chip factory (more than \$1 billion) and the intellectual capital required create barriers to entry that would be the envy of any executive. When you've got the Growth Attitude, though, you know that today's sales don't guarantee tomorrow's survival.

Andy Grove is intensely aware of this. To keep his billion-dollar factories running at capacity, he's got to convince customers to buy each new Intel innovation as fast as the company can turn them out. Already the business market has shown a reluctance to keep marching to the beat of perpetual upgrades—after all, how fast does a PC need to be to run a word processing package?

Grove's answer has been to work closely with Microsoft and promote the Windows NT operating system, which does require the next-generation chip. By making Windows 95 history, both Intel and Microsoft move back to the top of the down escalator. Grove has also sought to protect Intel's future by expanding into the consumer and workstation markets, even if that invites a collision with consumer giants like Sony or current customers such as Hewlett-Packard.

To accomplish the second goal, in 1989 Grove introduced the "Intel Inside" branding campaign with a \$5 million budget. At that time many wondered what he was doing. First, no high-tech company was using regular TV advertising. Second, image advertising for a component that no one would buy on its own was revolutionary. Most recently, Intel ads have dancing wafer-fabrication workers touting the virtues of the new MMX graphics technology.

Does it work? The results speak for themselves. As of June 1996, a few PC manufacturers (like Compaq, Dell, and Hewlett-Packard, all paranoid, speed demons in their own right) were making paper-thin margins, while most others (such as Digital Equipment and AST) were losing money. Competitor microprocessor companies such as AMD and Cyrix blow hot and cold, but Intel continues to chalk up record profits and earnings. Windows NT sales growth is propelling growth of the Pentium Pro, and studies report that consumer recognition of the Intel Inside logo now slightly exceeds that of the NutraSweet swirl. Paranoia keeps Intel moving, and winning.

———————

It's tempting to dismiss the Intel example as unique to high technology's fast pace. What about a traditionally slower-moving industry, such as publishing? Is the competitive paranoia and impatience of the Growth Attitude relevant here? Wayne Oler, CEO of International Thomson Publishing Education Group, certainly thinks so. Thomson is the largest higher-education publisher in the world, and surely few industries have been more broadly affected by the knowledge explosion, Oler uses his own version of pace and paranoia to drive growth and change.

The digital revolution is turning publishing upside down. In Oler's terms, publishers now have to think and: act "media neutral." The media container for information might be a CD-ROM, floppy diskette, video, direct download, or traditional paper, and that's just the beginning. Why does a textbook like Paul Samuelson's classic *Economics* have to be the same for each school, or professor? In today's digital world, the technology to create a custom version, tailored to the curriculum and each professor's unique teaching style, is possible. Why not integrate a video clip from "Wall Street Week" with Samuelson's text on a CD-ROM? What about two-way publishing? Combine the CD-ROM with an Internet-based discussion forum.

Until now, the publishing industry has lived on paper and ink. Oler's editors, marketers, designers, and production employees were all raised and educated in a world whose traditions go back to when monks wrote books by hand. They now find themselves thrown into a digital world with little knowledge of programming, multimedia software, the Internet, and more. Additionally, Oler now faces competitors that he's never raced against and, even worse, that already know how to play the new game. What's today's top-selling encyclopedia? No, it's not the World Book or the Britannica; they've been replaced by Microsoft's Encarta—available on CD-ROM at one-tenth the cost, and complete with video clips. Oler finds himself in a race that's just as heated and consequential as any in Silicon Valley.

Oler sees that he has to create a sense of crisis (or "burning platform," in his words), because his challenge is tougher than that of Intel's Grove. First, since publishing doesn't ride the Valley's down escalator, he can't rely on economic conditions to convey a sense of innovation urgency. Second, he has to exist in both the present and the future, because the legacy revenue stream from Thomson's traditional paper-based products provides the cash to create the new digital world. At the same time, Oler has to expand his people's skills, work processes, and business model to fight the digital battle. His challenge is the uncertainty of the cut-over. The question is not *will* publishing be revolutionized, but when?

How does Oler create the burning platform? He's quick to admit that it starts with himself. He's got to set the pace and keep the challenge in front of his people. He does this by constantly testing and exploring the dilemmas of opportunity and threat with employees every chance he gets. By raising the issue and calibrating the response, he knows where and when to turn up the flames.

Oler created "centers of excellence" at Thomson focused on the new technologies and competitive model. The centers provide a locus for experimentation; regular best-practice meetings cull and transfer learnings. Oler balances today's needs with tomorrow's by carefully gauging how many and what types of resources he throws at these new-world experiments. The centers provide an incubator not just for new skills and technologies, but also for fostering the Growth Attitude within his leadership team.

As a consequence of these efforts, editor's jobs have been redefined. Once upon a time, editors defined a need, found authors, and put together a business plan based on the cost and sales expectations for the life of an edition. Today they act more like Procter & Gamble brand managers. Oler's new value-focused model requires editors to define what will make this opportunity compelling and how it is differentiated from the competition through media, distribution, customization, or some other attribute.

When asked how essential is growth to Thomson, Oler responds as follows: "At the end of the day, I've got to stretch my organization's thinking, in ways it needs to be stretched, to stay light on its feet and close to the radical rate of change in the world today. If you don't set high growth targets, you don't develop the intellectual and physical prowess required to compete successfully."

2. Focus Externally: Get Everyone Looking Out

Silicon Valley leaders are constantly scanning their external environment, almost as though they were human radar dishes constantly looking for ideas, information, and opportunities. These leaders make rapid decisions, but what appears to outsiders as gunslinging or intuition is usually based on a rich, constantly refreshed database of tacit knowledge.

Valley leaders will also share with outsiders what more traditional firms keep to themselves. Why? To get feedback. so when they do pursue an innovation or partnership, they've got the right target and the best support they can. David Brown, former president of Quantum Corporation, used to share his firm's strategic plan with key customers and suppliers. Brown felt that this practice enhanced Quantum's position rather than compromised it. If customers or suppliers saw something in the strategy that didn't fit with their view of the future, they'd tell him in time to fix it. If they didn't know what the strategy was, though, they couldn't help.

Nothing destroys a rapidly growing Valley company's outward orientation as rapidly and insidiously as success. As the firm grows, the number of people who are in regular contact with the outside world shrinks drastically. In a firm of a thou-

FIGURE 3–1

Size Focuses People Inward

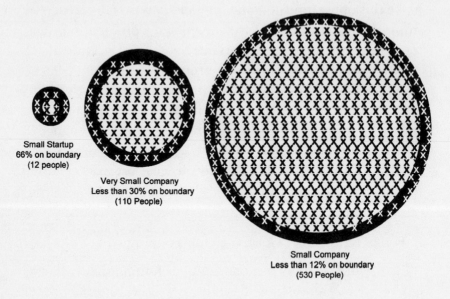

Small Startup
66% on boundary
(12 people)

Very Small Company
Less than 30% on boundary
(110 People)

Small Company
Less than 12% on boundary
(530 People)

sand people, only a small minority might have ongoing contact with customers, competition, suppliers, and the like; the rest spend their time interacting only with each other (see Figure 3–1). Colleagues quickly become friends. Though this fulfills the critical human need for community, it doesn't take very long before maintaining internal priorities and friendships becomes a priority. Just as differentiation is required for ecosystems to thrive, the same is true for innovation and growth.

Cisco System's John Chambers never stops pushing people to think of the customer. Once a year, Cisco conducts an independent customer satisfaction survey that measures fifty-five attributes. Chambers believes fervently that there is a direct correlation between customer satisfaction and growth/profitability, with a twelve-month lag. Accordingly, all Cisco managers have customer satisfaction goals as their primary performance and compensation measure. At Cisco, how you're doing "out there" is the basis for how well you're doing "in here." The forced exposure to outside views that results spurs innovation.

They don't play games with this commitment. Chambers told me that a Japanese customer had a problem regarding Cisco's hardware design. Some felt the Japanese making too much of a minor cosmetic flaw, but not Chambers. "We stick with what the customer defines as problems—and if they say it's a quality problem, then it is."

Why does Chambers feel so strongly? Perhaps another example will help explain. In the mid-1990s, customers rated their satisfaction with Cisco's software lower than other product and service dimensions. After an intense effort, the software scores improved, but the customer ratings didn't go up as much as Cisco's own internal quality measures. Some were upset, but Chambers and his team looked deeper. What they learned was that although customers had seen a tremendous improvement, the importance of software had also risen dramatically. It used to be an inconvenience if a local network went down for a while, but Cisco's customers pointed out that this was no longer true. With the entire organization now linked together, if the network went down, so did the business!

Jumping on an opportunity is easy for a small firm, but how do you do it when you've got 20,000 employees? Ask Bill Gates of Microsoft. After the dragstrip-style acceleration that took Netscape Communications from being an unknown startup to celebrity status, the coffee talk in the Valley was, "How did Microsoft miss the Internet?" (Everyone loves to kick the big guy when they've finally stumbled.) For our purposes, the more important question is, what can we learn from how fast and thoroughly Microsoft responded?

In the early 1990s, Microsoft was in the midst of a tremendous growth cycle, going from approximately $1.2 billion and 5,600 employees to $8 billion and 20,000 employees in 1997. When the Internet really began to soar, the firm was in the final stretch of its Windows 95 launch. A few voices within Microsoft advocated the need for an Internet strategy, but not a critical mass. In the late fall of 1995 with the massive launch behind them, Microsoft's leadership team looked at the Internet again and dramatically changed their tune. In the following six months, CEO Bill Gates did what few executives would consider—he changed Microsoft's entire business philosophy, dropped the Windows-centered view of computing to make winning on the Internet the new top priority. By June of 1996 Microsoft developed its own Web browser, persuaded America Online to adopt this browser over upstart Netscape's industry standard, distributed 90,000 copies of its Internet Information Server, acquired five companies to jumpstart various product efforts, and licensed archrival Sun's Java software in perhaps the ultimate "if you can't lick'em, join 'em" move. External focus and rapid realignment has enabled Microsoft to come from nowhere to become a leading Internet software provider.

3. Flatten the Organization and Blur Boundaries with Open, High-Velocity Information

The first step here has nothing to do with the boxes on the organization chart. Instead, it demands an attitude switch away from job descriptions, status, hierarchy, and above all else the infamous "need to know." In traditional organizations, information becomes currency that is hoarded at each succeeding level of hierarchy. In an economy based on knowledge, however, those without information can't contribute responsibly. In contrast, those with information find themselves compelled to act.

The Growth Attitude says *everyone* needs to know. Hewlett-Packard general managers hold regular cafeteria sessions with all employees to describe how the business is going, what the competition is up to, how this quarter's revenues look, and what staffers can do to help, followed by a wide-open question-and-answer session. With rare exceptions, most questions are answered directly and immediately. Five employees at Silicon Graphics publish a daily newspaper, Silicon Junction, over their company intranet. The paper focuses on key projects, customers, and issues, while sprinkling in other information about the Silicon Graphics community.

In fact, the SGI intranet is the backbone of the Silicon Graphics product design process. Web-based development begins with a series of concept papers that are electronically posted and available to all. As development moves forward, tools and templates that address the details of SGI's process are readily available. As CEO Ed McCracken describes it. "In the old organization, if you wanted more information to get the job done, you were a subversive. Managers used information to govern who was in and out of the loop, and of course the decisions." McCracken maintains his own home page, which contains copies of his most recent speeches to analysts or the press, as well as video clips. When people plagiarize his comments, McCracken is pleased no end.

Silicon Valley leaders with the Growth Attitude go far beyond what used to be called an open-door policy. If you were to sit in a meeting at most any Valley company, you'd be struck by the mix of people, expertise, and ages in the room. More importantly, you'd witness a degree of candor that's not typically found in hierarchical companies. In the more direct cultures, such as Sun Microsystems or Intel, you could easily walk in on a high-volume argument between a senior executive and an entry-level engineer. Status and seniority aren't based on age; they're based on what you know and can deliver.

4. Promoting People With Passion and Giving Them "Skin"

Have you ever been on a truly high-performing team? One that clicked like a hot jazz combo? If you have—and I hope so, because the experience is extraordinary—ask yourself, was it an emotional experience? Of the thousands of executives I've asked this question around the world, the answer is always an emphatic yes. When I ask these executives what made it emotional, their answers invariably include a description of prevailing through some crisis.

Emotion gets a bum rap. Despite talk about how emotions cloud our decision making, I'd argue that nothing is more important in knowledge work and leadership than having people who are passionate about their work. This passion fights against complacent behavior, which in turn creates me-too products and services. Inevitably, this passion can also fuel some very strong debates. Cirrus Logic's CEO Mike Hackworth excels at engaging in such debates. He keeps one channel of his mind wide open for any brilliance that might pop up while using another to manage the potential disruption. In Hackworth's mind, the latter is a small price to pay. If he shuts out the brilliance, he might as well shut down Cirrus Logic.

Many Fortune 100 companies mute or eliminate passion. They hire the brightest stars they can find, then spend the first few years of employment showing them how to "fit in" (in other words, conform) to the organization. Metaphorically, the goal is to chip off all the stars' points until they become perfect circles, at which point the company declares, "You're now one of us!" The passion that these stars might bring to the organization is lanced and drained as though it were an infection.

In contrast, finding and nurturing people with passion is so important to Valley leaders that they take hiring people very seriously. If you want a job at Cisco, SGI, Sun, Cirrus, or Quantum, you'd better get ready for no less than six and perhaps as many as twelve interviews with your prospective boss, co-workers, boss's peers, subordinates, and a key executive. Knowledge work thrives in a tight community—and before you ask someone to join, you'd better make sure most of the community wants him or her as well. This is a cultural fit and values test that follows the basic competence screening.

A by-product of passion (and competitive paranoia) is high expectations from everyone, including your peers. You'd better be a contributor, because no one has time for anything less. A "do what it takes" mentality makes for long hours, changed vacation schedules, and more than occasional burnout—a serious Silicon Valley issue. To compensate for the high stress, many Valley firms have sabbatical programs that kick in every four to six years.

The Valley also has a fair amount of leader-generated turnover that occurs in conjunction with down business cycles and the demands of growth. In contrast to some traditional firms that strive to minimize attrition, Valley companies use turnover as a way to reassess their people and upgrade them as necessary. Because jobs grow faster than capabilities in rapidly growing firms, Valley firms can't meet their managerial needs if they promote only from within. Hiring from the outside requires sensitivity and judgment, however, when internal candidates are turned down. Charles R. Schwab's president, Dave Pottruck, provides a useful rule of thumb for outside hires that works well: To get the job, the outside candidate clearly must be talented, as well as being someone from whom internal candidates would enjoy learning.

Passion is also tied to one's investment and consequences. Some people will always put in 110 percent simply because that's how they're built. Many more will put in that much if they have a significant investment in the outcome. In the Silicon Valley, people often describe this as "having some skin in the game." With a bias toward upside opportunity, Valley leaders use skin to motivate knowledge workers. One form of skin is the credibility associated with creating cutting-edge technology. Valley leaders and peers don't hesitate to glorify those who are behind the creation of new products and services, both internally and in the trade press. Such a reputation can ensure that you get to pick your next project (either in your current company or elsewhere).

Stock is by far the most common form of skin Valley leaders use. Stock options are very powerful for three reasons. First, the potential to accumulate significant wealth is real. Second, the value of the company's stock is directly tied to its ability to innovate consistently. Third, stock creates an "I am the company" sense of ownership. The key differences between the use of stock in the Silicon Valley and in most Fortune 100 companies is that in the Valley, the numbers and types of people who receive options are much broader.

5. Go for It: Set Stretch Goals, Make a Decision, and Make It Work (Or Learn What Will)

Valley leaders possess and express a sense of confidence in themselves and their organization's ability to learn. They have a healthy fear of failure, of course—they just don't equate it with death. When choosing between two alternatives, Quantum's David Brown is fond of saying, "Let's make the best decision we can, and then focus on making our decision work. If we're wrong, we'll find out and fix it."

Luck is a central element of growth and innovation. Look at the reemergence of Sun Microsystems due to its Java authoring software, which lets users attach small applications to World Wide Web pages. Was Java planned that way? Not at all; it was supposed to be an operating system for hand-held computers. By constantly analyzing both the environment and their project for other opportunities, Sun engineers turned what had become a stalled development effort into a corporate success story.

BUILDING ON THE GROWTH ATTITUDE

The Growth Attitude starts at the top. It happens because Silicon Valley leaders like Andy Grove breathe life into competitive paranoia with every decision and communication they make. Cisco Systems thrives on customer feedback because CEO John Chambers does. These actions establish a cadence throughout the management ranks that spurs relentless growth and innovation. By itself, however, the Growth Attitude is incomplete. Just as even the best motivated football team needs a game plan, so does a company. What makes successful Valley leaders remarkable is their ability to both generate and reach beyond the Growth Attitude.

Silicon Valley workers, like those elsewhere, thrive on leadership, but they have an increasingly low tolerance for being managed. When you err these days, you're quickly labeled a "micromanager" (regardless of your intentions), and become grist for a future Dilbert cartoon. The challenge facing leaders has never been more formidable: How do you create cohesion among a global community of educated people who are increasingly mobile and likely to be experts in their own right? Stated slightly differently, how do Valley leaders balance motivational leadership and sound business management to keep all these pumped-up independent thinkers pointed in the same direction and working toward the same goals?

In many respects, the challenge facing these leaders is not unique. There are five key questions to which they must provide coherent answers, either directly or through others:

- Where are we going?
- How are we going to get there?
- What do we need to get there?
- How are we organized/structured?
- How do we detect and correct our course?

Valley leaders differ from others, though, in that they actively seek input for answering these questions outside the traditional management hierarchy. To characterize their behavior as participative would be too broad, for they are very targeted in who they personally seek out. They tend to look to their leading technical thinkers and successful managers (for example, as one who's just introduced a hot new product). These people are closest to the pulse of the technology and marketplace. Additionally, Valley leaders don't artificially elevate their management role above others. While top managers' impact is certainly broader, their tasks are not considered any more or less important than those of the person who runs the customer service center.

Answering the above questions with action is the essence of business leadership:

1. Establish a clear, compelling purpose, direction, and set of goals
2. Define a competitive strategy and ensure its execution and adoption
3. Secure and develop resources: knowledge, people, and financial
4. Architect organization structures and process that are aligned with purpose, strategy, resources, and capability
5. Lead organizational learning and change

Let's see how Valley leaders address each task, with a focus on what's unique about their leadership approach.

1. Establish a Clear, Compelling Purpose, Direction, and Set of Goals

Regardless of how intensely or frequently knowledge workers might question the direction chosen, it remains the leader's job to define that direction and convey how it supports the fundamental purpose of the unit or organization. Silicon Valley leaders engage individuals and groups in an ongoing dialogue that tests the correctness of their choices, but they do not transfer the responsibility for choosing—that is abdication, not participation.

Innovation leadership requires a visionary purpose and goals. Valley innovators want to be the first, the best, or the most elegant solution providers; simply providing an alternative product or service with no serious differentiation from its competitors is not compelling. Just as the presence of the Growth Attitude sets a contagious tone, when Valley leaders stretch the imaginations of their people, the definition of what is possible rises with each new innovation. This element of leadership has a very personal dimension, for if leaders are not excited by their own vision, it is doubtful that others will be. Steve Jobs epitomized this dimension as he drove Apple to create "insanely great" products during the development of the Macintosh. His infectious passion was clearly reflected in the product.

How much you involve others in the search for direction is a personal choice. Firms such as Oracle have been extraordinarily successful behind the vision of a powerful leader like Larry Ellison, while others (including Sun) have elegantly orchestrated a collective vision that is equally compelling. Incorporate any and all input that makes the purpose and direction come alive, but don't incorporate items just because they make it more acceptable to others. Make sure you keep stretch in your vision—because when you take out the stretch, you often take out the power.[2] The constant tension between today's reality and your goals is what spurs extraordinary innovation.

Valley leaders communicate purpose and direction consistently and within multiple contexts. They aren't shy about injecting the color and passion that brought the vision to life when they share their thinking; the communication should be as enduring as the firm's passion and purpose. Like the famous Energizer bunny that keeps going and going, Valley leaders need to resurface constantly to test purpose and direction. That way each encounter people have with the firm's vision unveils another element or connection, just as if they are listening to a favorite song or watching a favorite movie. In addition, Valley leaders keep linking the events of today to their vision, underscoring the relationship between the two. Emphasizing the importance of today's work keeps people focused, while linking it to the vision keeps them motivated.

2. Define a Competitive Strategy; Ensure Its Execution and Adoption

These leaders use strategy to communicate how the firm will win within the intensely competitive Silicon Valley. Workers

do not accept their company's strategy, though, without testing it against their understanding of the market, competition,
and technology. One pitfall of this is that some employees may
value bold technical innovation over incremental change,
often to a fault. If technical people don't have sufficient exposure to the rationale behind the nontechnical elements of the
strategy, for example, they can resist by pushing their narrow
view longer than is helpful.

As the knowledge required for Valley companies to compete
increases, we're seeing a fundamental change in how strategy
is defined. Because the complexity and speed of change make it
increasingly unlikely that any group of executives has sufficient
knowledge to define strategy on their own, it's increasingly
common for executives to establish some broad direction, a
strawman, and then involve the rest of the organization in
defining and refining key strategic thrusts. This is how leaders
at Cisco Systems, Cirrus Logic, and Silicon Graphics approach
strategy. The resulting system-wide learning environment generates alignment as well as defining direction.

This is a parallel process, not a bottom-up one. As different
geographies and business units define and forward their
thoughts, top management tests each against their own. This
is followed by a compare-and-contrast period wherein all par-
ties react to what the others have done. Senior management
focuses on overall strategy, looking for congruence and leverage and testing the degree of stretch present. The business
units take in what other units are doing, incorporate senior
management's perspective, and reassess their own thinking.

In the Valley, the medium for dialogue often focuses on
product roadmaps, which define new product and service initiatives within a market and technology context (see Figure
3–2). While one could argue that those should be an outcome
of strategy discussions, it's difficult to separate the chicken
from its egg so neatly. Starting with product roadmaps provides a degree of tangibility that helps bring other choices in
direction, technology, distribution, and so forth to the sur-

FIGURE 3-2

Parallel Planning Process

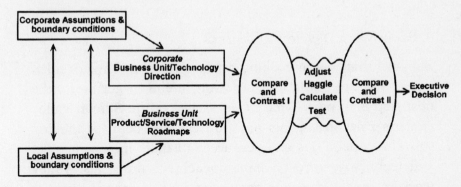

face. Furthermore, it forces people to be explicit about how their ideas translate into new products or services.

Certainly in high tech, but also for other manufacturing businesses, the product roadmap embodies a large percentage of the strategy. If you use this approach, though, it's absolutely vital that your conversation discovers the assumptions beneath the selection of products. If the discussion stays at the level of comparing products and features without exploring the underlying rationale, it will have significantly less strategic value.

The Valley's open strategy process is powerful for several reasons. First, it involves more of the total organization knowledge base into the strategy development process than the executives can do themselves. Second, it provides senior knowledge workers with an opportunity to influence and understand the choices (and consequences) facing the firm, creating useful engagement while reducing after-the-fact potshots. Third, it transforms the serial process of defining and executing strategy into a concurrent development and deployment process. People get exposed to the rationale for strategy elements outside their expertise, then have the opportunity to challenge, contribute to, and digest them. Fourth, when it comes time to broadly communicate and implement the final strategy, companies that use this process start with an established critical mass.

3. Secure and Develop Resources

Suppose that you are taking a trip. After you have decided where you are going and how you intend to get there, the next step is to pack. That's the essence of the Silicon Valley leader's role once goals and strategy are defined: making sure the capabilities and resources (usually money, people, and technology) are on hand to achieve the goals. Valley workers quickly become frustrated if they spend much of their time fighting the bureaucracy for resources. They certainly need to be involved in defining resource and capability requirements, but it's up to leaders to ensure these are delivered. When they do that, leaders soon find themselves with a lot of friends.

It's useful to break the leader's role regarding resources into near- and long-term responsibilities. The near-term focus is to ensure that innovation projects have the required resources available when they need them. In the Silicon Valley and elsewhere, projects rarely start with the staffing that everyone agrees is necessary, if only because people usually believe that getting started is better than doing nothing. When you start a brand-new initiative without key resources, though, the chances of having to backpedal and retrace your steps once they become available are very high.

The root cause of this problem is that firms regularly take on more projects than they have the capability to execute. Because most launch innovation initiatives as ideas emerge and needs arise, the cumulative demand (particularly on support resources) is invisible. Furthermore, assumptions about what is required are usually optimistic, even though the best-case scenario is rarely achieved.

Despite this tendency to overload workers and underestimate needs, however, Silicon Valley leaders are particularly adroit at partnering for resources. With knowledge in all disciplines growing at exponential rates, Valley leaders pick and choose (1) what their firm uniquely does that creates a competitive advantage; 2) what's required to be superb, but is outside their capabilities; and 3) what's required, but offers little differentiation. Valley leaders focus their firm's resources on what it does best and what creates competitive advantage. The small amount of cost savings that doing other tasks might bring is weighed against the distraction and investments that will be required to stay up to date over time.

In the longer term, Silicon Valley leaders continually assess, redefine, and then secure the core competencies that they must have to compete. A core competency does three things.[3] First, it makes a disproportionate contribution to customer value—in the case of Silicon Graphics (SGI), its skills at 3D visual computing are a prime example. Second, the competency should open doors to other opportunities just as SGI's 3D technology did in cinematic special effects and animation. Third, the competency should represent such a blend of tacit and explicit knowledge that it cannot be copied easily. Defining and developing a critical mass of capabilities is a constant challenge since the available knowledge keeps growing exponentially; what you can do is always dwarfed by what you want to do.

Valley technical and human resource leaders constantly scan the environment for auxiliary capabilities within the supplier and university communities, initiating alliances so that everything is lined up when help is required. Both of these tasks require a tight link to strategy, and they are why a strong human resources department is worth its weight in gold.

Let me restate that although the Silicon Valley certainly is driven by technology, required competence extends beyond technical know-how. Both Quantum and Cirrus Logic found that when they moved to a flatter organization, they had plenty of top-flight technologists but far too few technology managers. These managers are skilled technologists who also value the contribution from other functions, and who play an active role integrating these functions during the innovation process.

4. Architect and Align Organization Structures and Processes

Whether they are designing a new building, a new service business, or an electronic circuit, the best architects supplement functionality with a sense of style and artistic genius that makes their efforts special. Elegant designs create boundaries that channel resources and energy, as well as providing contact points or intersections where you'd naturally expect them. Organization and process architectures work the same way.

There is no such thing, however, as a perfect organization design. Choices that make it easy to do one thing make it harder to do something else. For example, if intimate contact with the customer is your most important goal, then a market-focused business unit structure may be your best choice. This same structure, though, also makes it more difficult to develop deep expertise in functional skills. With functional resources spread across the business units, it will be tough for employees to define a career path and exchange ideas and learning. What differentiates Silicon Valley leaders from others is they design (and continually redesign) their firm's organizational and process architecture to make innovation a path of least resistance.

During a top management meeting in the fall of 1988, Quantum's executives complained about how their archcompetitor, Conner Peripherals, was winning customers with products that were inferior in performance and quality. The critical difference was that Conner's products were available three months or more before Quantum's. Over the next three years, it was decided, Quantum's strategic focus would be speed.

The Quantum organization was structured around traditional functional lines (read: silos), with a corresponding "over the wall" serial product development process. As a first step toward improvement, the top brass created strong multifunctional teams to develop products and manage each of Quantum's core markets. Concurrently, the firm's leaders analyzed their product development process, looking for barriers to speed. They found that development programs often drifted because there weren't clearly defined decision makers. Quantum redesigned the development process with clear decision roles for team members and functional experts.

The results were rapid and significant. Issues that once had to filter their way to the executive staff for resolution were now settled within the teams or at lower functional levels. Drifting decisions found homes. Over the course of three years, disk drives that used to take as long as thirty months to develop began showing up in half that time.

While implementing its new approach, Quantum learned that few of its people had strong functional skills *and* could work in the new multifunctional environment. A brief discussion was held: Did the new organization require a rare set of skills that could not be obtained, or was the gap simply a reflection of Quantum's past? Quickly concluding that the problem was a holdover from the past, the leaders dramatically changed the company's hiring priorities and procedures. The sum of these actions aligned Quantum's structure, process, and capacity with its strategy.

5. Lead Organizational Learning and Change

Innovation is an interesting paradox. On the one hand, you've got to grow a rich knowledge base to compete. On the other, the more knowledge you have, the greater your chances are of becoming trapped by it. Remember what I said about how success can stifle an organization's growth because the employees begin serving each other rather than the customer? The same is true with innovation. Companies can quickly become arrogant about what they know, losing sight of what they need to learn.

Silicon Valley leaders focus on three dimensions of learning and change. First, they make sure the firm searches for and ingests new knowledge from outside, through either partnership or acquisition. Unlike other areas of the country, the core purpose of Valley acquisitions is to capture additional knowledge. Cirrus Logic purchased Crystal Semiconductor for its analog technology, for example, and Quantum bought Digital Equipment's drive business to gain access to the latter's magneto-resistive recording head technology.

Second, Valley leaders create mechanisms that capture, appraise, and recirculate knowledge that is generated within the firm. Internal technical conferences are quite common, with the focus on knowledge exchange and best-practice identification. Larger companies such as Hewlett-Packard have internal technical journals that rival those from top universities. Informal networks, intranets, and e-mail are also actively used.

Third, Valley leaders spearhead the process of discarding knowledge that is no longer useful. How do they do this? First, they embrace young people and their ideas. For example, many college students create and maintain their own personal Web pages on the Internet, complete with animation and music. How many forty-year-old engineers can do that? In contrast to traditional notions of seniority, Valley leaders rely on their young people and give them far more responsibility than other firms. My personal observation is that the average age of a director-level individual in the Valley is at least five and often ten years younger than his or her counterpart in traditional firms.

Valley leaders make investments in a wide variety of technologies. Rather than trying to guess which will win, these leaders will invest limited amounts in several, either internally or externally. In addition, they have their own robust peer network that keeps them in touch with venture capitalists and new startups. Valley leaders invest a portion of their earnings in these startups; for example, Intel has investments in more than fifty new companies with a total value of $500 million.

Investing in tools that speed the flow of knowledge into and around their firm is also common. Groupware, such as

Lotus Notes or intranets, is broadly deployed to create a backbone for explicit knowledge. While most of us rarely tap the power that's available in our hand-held calculator, Silicon Valley firms are at the leading edge of how to use groupware effectively. Besides electronic tools, Valley leaders partner with universities and research centers (such as the Institute for the Future and the MIT Center for Organizational Learning) to define work methodologies that both deepen and speed up knowledge creation.

All of this work starts within the leader. A characteristic of CEOs in stagnant Silicon Valley companies (often referred to as the "living dead") is that they ask their people to innovate and grow but do not do so themselves. If people see that the boss is a "know-it-all," at the very best they'll be motivated to learn all the boss knows. If the boss has a rich sense of curiosity that openly questions the impact of not only his actions but those of others, the business, and competitors, then others will learn from this and do likewise.

Valley leaders constantly test the continued validity of their knowledge and business paradigms. Ask yourself, are you devoting thoughtful energy to learning, or do you assume it just happens because you're intelligent, active, and aware? Do you only go public once you've made a decision, or do you engage others in learning with you? Let's close our look at Valley leadership to see how a traditional firm, Emerson Electric, blended the Growth Attitude with these leadership practices and adapted them to its business in order to drive growth through innovation.

HOW EMERSON ELECTRIC INJECTED THE GROWTH ATTITUDE INTO HEAVY MANUFACTURING

For the last fifteen years, Emerson Electric's CEO, Chuck Knight, has pushed his organization to be the best-cost producer. Emerson has racked up thirty-nine years of consecutive dividend and earnings increases and grown to over $11 billion, a record of which any company would be justly proud. In the 1990s, though, Knight saw that gains from efficiencies were reaching the point of diminishing returns, and Wall Street wouldn't improve Emerson's market valuation without seeing double-digit growth. Besides, constantly cutting and squeezing costs isn't much fun. Although Emerson had become quite skilled at acquisitions over the years, Knight believed that he couldn't attain double-digit growth without innovation, and that would take some doing.

As a strong and very visible leader, the first thing Knight did was change his public behavior. He did this by setting an aggressive target—35 percent of sales would come from products introduced in the last five years—changing management success criteria, and constantly communicating the new objectives. He changed what he placed on the agenda at corporate planning meetings during board-level discussions and even before external analysts. Growth and innovation topics pushed out some of the operating analysis and detail. Perhaps most importantly, he openly attacked what many considered as sacred Emerson practices, declaring that they were no longer doing the job.

In conjunction with Charlie Peters, vice president of technology and development, Knight established a plan for turning his new message into practice. Emerson is renowned for its internal planning processes;[4] Knight uses a series of annual operations planning conferences, as his way of influencing what is otherwise a highly decentralized company. To signal the importance of growth through innovation, Knight initiated annual growth conferences, thereby leveraging a familiar practice to get his leaders to pay attention.

By separating operations and planning, he was able to sustain Emerson's core strengths in profit planning and operations while introducing fundamentally new assumptions relative to innovation. Using the conference format also enabled him to make sure that each company was rigorous in its innovation and growth plans, ensuring that initiatives were crisply defined and could be tracked. At the same time, Knight added new assumptions, tools, and formats to the growth conference that encouraged people to think outside their operations heritage. For example, he encouraged broader participation in conference planning from functions such as sales and development.

A couple of years into the growth initiative, Knight and others began to uncover barriers that they hadn't seen at the start. First, additional investments in skills were required in areas that surprised him. He expected that more engineers would be needed, but often it was the lack of marketing talent to help define new products that was missing. Adding more engineers only exacerbated the problem, because without additional marketing capability, new programs were either stalled or launched with definitions that didn't meet customer requirements. Knight used consultants and training to augment and upgrade skills.

Second, Knight found that the plethora of measures that enabled them to thread the needle on cost didn't provide useful data for innovation. He responded by adding measures that examined cycle time, development capacity, and productivity. Third, as you might expect, Knight was quickly hit with requests for more resources from nearly every company. The mindset of many company presidents was that growth through innovation was additive to the existing business model, and therefore more resources were needed. This quickly became a major issue.

One of the reasons that company presidents were pushing for more resources is that they wanted to start as many innovations as they could right away to make sure they achieved the five-year goal. This skewed the true resource requirements to the front end. In addition, their lack of experience with leading and managing innovation made them blind to potential productivity inefficiencies within their innovation programs. Knight agreed to a significant number of resource requests, but he also provided outside consulting support to clarify innovation strategy and process productivity while injecting some realism into what resources were truly required and when.

The results of Knight's efforts are compelling. Starting from a dead stop in 1994, Emerson is on target to reach the 35 percent goal. Like that of Thomson's Oler, Knight's market environment doesn't ignite the paranoia that drives innovation as occurs in Silicon Valley; he had to create his burning platform with the help of education, internal goals, and Wall Street's unwillingness to improve the company's valuation without it. Through the growth conference format and added marketing and consulting support, he did get company presidents to look outside much more than they had in the past. Have they developed the passion of the Growth Attitude? Knight certainly has. In last year's growth conference, he closed by telling his leaders that while there were plenty of challenges before them, he hadn't had so much fun in years!

4

Strategy in a
$20 Billion Startup

Do you have any middle-aged friends who take life on as though they were ten years younger than they really are—the sports nuts, for example, who try to keep up with the college kids on the ski slopes or tennis courts? Perhaps they had a great youth and see no reason to stop, or are scared to death of aging, or both. If we apply this same perspective to corporations, it wouldn't be a bad description of many companies in the Silicon Valley. Former startups like Sun Microsystems and Cirrus Logic may not have the spry quickness that comes naturally when you're young, but they still remember their startup days and try to act like it.

This lingering startup mentality colors the way many Valley companies define and deploy their innovation strategy. Just as startups begin with an idea for a product or service rather than a comprehensive business strategy, innovation strategy development in Valley companies is an outgrowth of their product and service plans, not the reverse. These plans are idea driven, with available numbers added later as a san-ity check. In the best cases, these plans cover two product or service generations (usually a period of three years or less). Although this approach is not without problems, it *does* get to the essence of value creation and growth through innovation—ensuring a continuous flow of profitable new products and services.

In this chapter I'll tackle strategic alignment, the second element of the innovation model. Strategic alignment has two parts. The first is picking the right set of innovation initiatives, or what I call the portfolio; the second is making sure that your organization is aligned and capable of executing what you've chosen. Of the five elements in the model, strategic alignment is the element where leaders roll up their sleeves and do the most hands-on work. For that reason, you'll find this chapter is more detailed than others. My intent is to give you a roadmap and tools, while acknowledging that an entire book could be devoted to the subject.

I'll begin by defining the logic that Silicon Valley firms use to guide strategy development and execution. Next I will provide an overview of the portfolio approach and define the key parameters Valley companies use to assess and align their innovation portfolios. While doing this, I'll also underscore where Valley companies diverge from traditional approaches to strategy. I will then introduce you to NetDrive, Inc. (a fictional amalgam of Silicon Valley experience), where you'll get a chance to visit with a management team as they put their portfolio together and test it for alignment. Along the way, I'll provide you with tools that make building the portfolio easier and more effective.

VALLEY LEADERS USE FUZZY LOGIC FOR THE FUZZY FRONT END

The early phase of the innovation process is ripe with opportunity, but it is also devoid of many definitive facts. Rather than looking for answers, the best Silicon Valley leaders try to define the critical questions. Due to its high degree of ambiguity, this phase has become known as "the fuzzy front end."[1] On average, Valley leaders distinguish themselves from traditional managers by their ability to work within the ambiguity *without* rushing to remove it. It is from this ambiguity that opportunity emerges.

This practice parallels advice that Elliott Jacques, a brilliant Canadian management theorist, suggested years ago.[2] Jacques argues that the higher your position is, the longer the time should be from the moment you make a decision until you know whether it was a good one (Figure 4–1). For example, a floor supervisor in a restaurant may elect to close a section early one evening; if a large crowd shows up unexpectedly, he or she will know very quickly that this wasn't a good decision. Contrast this with the Valley executive who has to choose which of two immature, competing technologies to pursue. Assuming the time to develop and introduce the product or service is two years, the executive who makes this decision will have to wait at least 24 months to know if he or she was right.

When leaders delay their participation until the fuzzy front end disappears, they drift to a lower decision altitude (Figure 4–2). This may feel safer, but then leaders aren't adding incremental value. In effect, they simply duplicate (or, more likely,

FIGURE 4–1

Balanced Leadership

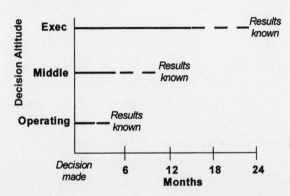

FIGURE 4-2

Reactive Leadership

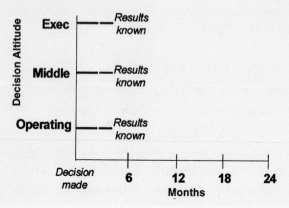

confuse) those who should be operating at that level. We've all been at meetings where multiple levels of management were present, but everyone operated at the same level, using the identical time horizon. One way that Silicon Valley leaders avoid this awkward situation is by using the managerial equivalent of fuzzy logic.

While the situations that fuzzy logic addresses are ambiguous, fuzzy logic itself is a very defined methodology. It's currently used to control appliances such as toasters, where "dark toast" cannot be defined by a single shade of brown. Valley leaders have an analogous form of logic that they use to address the ambiguity of the fuzzy front end. Influenced by the Growth Attitude, the following guidelines outline the core elements of this approach:

1. *The map is not the territory.* Silicon Valley leaders know that whatever plan they create will not be the one that they ultimately implement. Whether the market turns, a new technology surprises them, or something else unexpected occurs, these leaders know that they will have to take detours that aren't on their strategic roadmaps.

2. *Having a map is better than not having one.* When a company runs into an obstacle without a map, it's pretty

tough to know which way to turn. Having a collective understanding of business context and intentions enables Valley leaders to select and communicate alternate directions knowledgeably and quickly. That's the real value of a plan—when you need to turn left rapidly, everyone knows what left means.

3. *You'll never have all the data.* Valley leaders know that there will always be more information available tomorrow, and the day after that, and so on. Valley leaders know that this seductive but deadly cycle of waiting for more data can go on indefinitely. Besides, they understand that much of what is called data (such as market research) is more opinion than fact. Ask yourself whatever happened to pen-based computing—the so-called next revolution in computing?

4. *Ongoing thinking and action brings strategy to life.* Valley leaders build as much consensus as they can around the market, competition, and technology, picking a direction but never turning off their radar. Their constant scanning for new developments enables them to retarget briskly when needed. They know that locking into any plan when the competitive context continues to change is a foolish approach.

5. *One-off thinking yields one-off products.* Over time, Valley leaders have learned that one-off projects, even when successful, are very expensive. One-off projects live by themselves, with little connection to past or future efforts, and require more energy, specialized skills, and tools from every corner of the firm. The best leaders think in terms of product and service families, such as Intel's line of microprocessors.

6. *Find a partner.* No one goes it alone in the Silicon Valley. The important questions are, who do you do it with, what is the goal, and how is the deal structured? Valley companies focus internally or where they can make a world class contribution and then leverage the development risk, investment, and reward with others who can

bring their skills to the party. With partnering such a strong norm, a Valley company's capabilities, capacity, and accountability only begin inside the office walls.

7. *Listen to your current customers, but don't always believe them.* Often the benefits of new technology move faster than your current customers are willing to accept. Valley firms balance current customer input with their own understanding of the technology's potential. They also remember that although customers can be overly conservative, technology push by itself rarely wins.

8. *Money isn't everything.* Silicon Valley companies have learned that measuring return, risk, and investment solely in terms of dollars is a mistake. Capabilities grow through use, and how fast they grow is critical. The time required to learn a technology, or a market like the Internet, means you might be better jumping into a market before the financial returns meet your requirements.

With these ground rules in mind, let's look at why Silicon Valley leaders use a portfolio to manage innovation, what parameters they use to build and assess their portfolios, and how the fictional NetDrive builds its innovation portfolio.

WHY SILICON VALLEY COMPANIES USE AN INNOVATION PORTFOLIO

Valley firms use the portfolio approach for four reasons. First, the portfolio is a risk management tool. These firms typically have more innovation initiatives under way than traditional firms, and they are prone to stretch farther within each initiative. Without an overall view of their innovation efforts, they could easily wind up taking too much or too little risk. Additionally, using an innovation portfolio makes it easier to apportion risk between factors such as technology, markets, and distribution. A portfolio also provides visibility to the total risk as well as that within each initiative; having some conservative initiatives lets you stretch further in others. When a portfolio is not used, there is a tendency to require all projects to meet the same risk profile.

Second, the portfolio provides visibility that allows firms to pace the introduction of new products and services. Silicon Valley companies balance the introduction of revolutionary products with incremental, improvements in others so as to maintain a steady flow. By having a comprehensive view of their initiatives over time, they can avoid either overwhelming or underwhelming the marketplace. For example, Intel adjusts the rate at which they introduce new microprocessors (such as the Pentium) based on the margins they can get for their existing products. Their portfolio provides visibility across products and product generations, enabling them to maximize the profits they reap from each one.

Third, just as a radar screen enables air traffic controllers to sequence takeoffs and landings efficiently, the innovation portfolio helps Silicon Valley leaders time when they start a new initiative or transfer a completed one into manufacturing or the marketplace. Without a view across all products, Valley firms could easily find themselves in a situation where three new products enter the factory at the same time.

Fourth, the portfolio illuminates potential leverage opportunities among technologies, products, and markets. This capability enables Valley firms to get more for each innovation dollar while reducing development cost and risk. For example, every electrical product (from computers to test equipment) requires a power supply. Years ago, designing a power supply was the rite of passage for recently hired entry-level engineers. As Hewlett-Packard and other firms with large product lines grew, they began to proliferate power supply designs, with little value added for the customer. Several years ago, H-P looked across its product lines and quickly saw that it could very effectively support its business with 80 percent fewer power supply designs. Not only do such insights reduce complexity, they also free up people to work on

FIGURE 4–3

Initiative Type and Resources Versus Net Income

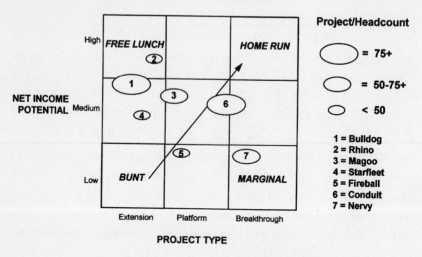

tasks that generate greater customer value. This becomes increasingly critical as the cost and risk of innovation rises.

In many ways, the portfolio approach is little more than applied common sense. Silicon Valley companies who use it well do not just make a list of initiatives; they create charts that compare them across dimensions such as risk, strategic fit, potential return, and resource requirements. An example, shown in Figure 4–3, compares project type and head count with net income potential. By using different charts as lenses to compare initiatives, Silicon Valley firms can mix and match alternatives until they come up with the portfolio that's right for them.

CREATING AND ASSESSING
THE INNOVATION PORTFOLIO

The key question facing every Valley company, though, is how do you ensure that you have the right initiatives in your portfolio? Besides assessing each initiative individually for risk, investment, return, and timing, firms use three primary criteria to assess their total portfolio:

1. *Stretch and strategic fit.* How much does the portfolio push the industry frontiers, and how well does it fit with their business goals and strategy?
2. *Capabilities and capacity.* Do they have the required capabilities to execute the portfolio and do they have enough of them?
3. *Leverage and risk.* Have they leveraged their investments so that they have a productivity advantage, while keeping risk within acceptable bounds?

Stretch and Strategic Fit

Deciding how much stretch to put into any individual project—and the portfolio at large—is an art, not a science. *Stretch* is shorthand for the degree of advancement from the current technology, process, market, or distribution. Stretch is relative to the competition, and more is not always better. American companies have both excelled and hung themselves by trying for more stretch in each innovation than they were capable of doing. In contrast, the Japanese tend to err on the side of incremental improvements, and in so doing often miss new technologies and markets.

Apple provides us with examples of too much stretch in the case of the Newton, and too little stretch in the evolution of the Macintosh. The Newton's problem was twofold. First, the product was ahead of the market. Having a potentially wireless hand-held device that was marginally better than an electronic organizer did not create a winning value proposition. The infrastructure required to provide additional benefit from wireless services did not exist at the Newton's introduction, and it still doesn't today. As often happens in the Silicon Valley, the product was a technology in search of a market, rather than the reverse. Second, and more central to its failure, the Newton was promoted as having high-quality handwriting recognition, but this feature did not have enough reliability to be useful. The product became the butt of jokes, including a series of ridiculing Doonesbury comic strips.

Too little stretch over the evolution of the Macintosh has nearly destroyed Apple. When first introduced, the Mac represented a tremendous improvement over existing MS-DOS computers. The addition of the mouse for selecting and drawing objects, combined with the graphical user interface, were significant advances. The problem is that since its introduction in the early 1980s, the Mac has remained relatively unchanged. During the introduction of Microsoft's Windows 95, Apple advertisements proclaimed that Windows 95 was no better than the Macintosh of 1989—unfortunately, neither were the newest Macintoshes. By failing to stretch its lead in user friendliness, Apple seriously wounded itself.

How do Silicon Valley firms decide if their portfolio has enough stretch? First, they assess the overall balance between revolutionary and evolutionary initiatives. Valley leaders constantly ask, if we execute our portfolio properly, where will this position us a year or two from today? In addition to asking this question internally, Valley executives test their portfolios through their network of contacts, augmented with venture capitalist briefings, analysts' reports, trade shows, and technical conferences. In the open Silicon Valley environment, the real challenge is learning not just what others are working on but what level of success they've achieved. When the day is done, the ultimate arbitrator of portfolio stretch is the leaders' judgment, experience, and luck.

Valley firms also constantly monitor technology developments that are independent of product and service initiatives. The best companies maintain roadmaps that define the next technologies they will pursue and the requisite timing of each. These technology roadmaps are matched to their product roadmaps to ensure that the two are synchronized; at least two generations of technologies, products, and services are always tracked. When new technologies mature faster than expected, Valley firms are not shy about shifting resources to exploit them—as Microsoft did when it jumped on the Internet bandwagon.

The technology roadmaps not only identify technologies but

define a migration path from one to another, as well as within the company. For example, computer firms continually try to reduce the number of chips in their products, usually by combining two or three chips into one. New application-specific chips (ASICs) are often introduced in a low-end product where the cost advantage has the most value. Once the chips are debugged and mature, they migrate to mid-range and high-end products. Such migration paths are shown on their technology roadmap in Figure 4–4.

Core technology developments that take longer, such as the pens in inkjet printers, are separated from shorter product and service initiatives. Hewlett-Packard maintains a separate division for pen development and supplies that feeds into the divisions that design the printers. By separating research and invention from product and service development, Silicon Valley companies can achieve stretch without incurring too much risk. For example, Hewlett-Packard's deskjet printer division spent several years trying to develop a new pen simultaneously with a new printer. Difficulties completing the pen eventually forced H-P to release the product with the past-generation pen. Although the derivative was not very

FIGURE 4–4

Technology Road Map

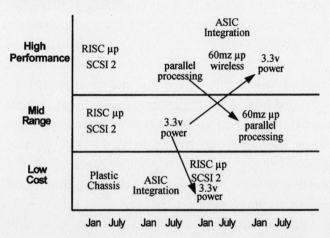

satisfying to those involved, it became a best-seller in the market.

Valley firms use a modular product/service architecture to isolate stretch in new products and services. Each pen Hewlett-Packard creates is used in several printer lines, thus leveraging the development effort across multiple products and markets. An additional advantage of this approach is that by carrying forward a significant portion of the prior product, H-P can isolate risk, reduce cost, and increase reliability.

Deciding how much stretch is required for strategic fit is where the Silicon Valley sharply departs from traditional companies. In the traditional firm, business strategy often precedes (or at least is claimed to precede) product and service innovation strategy. In the Valley the process is usually concurrent, and sometimes it is reversed. Frequently, corporate strategy is expressed in very high-level terms or is virtually non-existent. There are defined growth goals and target markets, but frequently little else.

Why does the Valley operate this way? Because its management structures are relatively flat and participatory; the information needed to define new innovation initiatives is distributed throughout the organization. Product and service plans define strategy, concurrently with strategy defining product and service plans. Rather than in-depth strategic scenarios or strategy papers, you're more likely to find a few simple statements that establish the boundaries for each firm's competitive efforts. Thus, strategy may appear to be an outcome of innovation planning, when it actually occurs in parallel.

Does this work? The results speak for themselves. The financial track record of Silicon Valley firms as innovators and wealth creators is unparalleled. Furthermore, the Valley approach parallels the ideas of Michael Porter, one of the world's leading strategy experts. Porter asserts that the essence of strategy is choosing what *not* to do more than what to do.[3] Porter further suggests that the activities that people undertake to create, produce, and deliver new products and services are the basic units of competitive advantage. Since the Valley lives and breathes by innovation, focusing on the development of technology and innovation planning engages people in exactly the work Porter describes.

When the Valley approach fails, it's frequently because leaders engage in hyperreactiveness, or what a colleague of mine refers to as "left rudder–right rudder" thinking. Rather than following a course until there is a significant reason to change, some Silicon Valley companies flail as they continuously react to the latest market or technological trend. In these firms, product and service definitions change with each piece of news, creating an endless loop changing direction, trying to catch up, changing direction, and trying to catch up again as innovation teams grapple with the "strategy du jour." The key to avoiding such shallow or short-term thinking is to surface and test the assumptions that drive new products and service decisions as you make these choices.

Achieving the right balance between stretch and strategic fit is the first test for any innovation portfolio. There would be little value in executing a portfolio that turned out new products and services which failed to provide sufficient value to attract additional customers. Let's now turn to how you assess the portfolio for sufficient capabilities and capacity.

Capabilities and Capacity

In the early 1980s I was an executive at Zilog Corporation— the creator of the Z80 microprocessor, the one-time leading microprocessor in the world. When shifting from the 8-bit Z80 to the 16-bit Z8000, Zilog decided to use a new product architecture that rendered existing Z80 software worthless. This was perhaps one of the most costly examples of technology push in Silicon Valley history for it not only destroyed Zilog as a player in the microprocessor industry but helped create Intel's virtual monopoly. As Zilog slipped further and further behind, the strategy suggestions from marketing became increasingly outlandish. It wasn't that the strategy itself

was internally flawed; rather, the strategy did not fit the capabilities of the company. It would have been a good strategy if
Zilog had the same resources as Intel, but we didn't.

In the fifteen years since Zilog's blunder, experience has
taught Valley leaders that no strategy or innovation portfolio
is meaningful if you don't possess the capabilities and capacity to execute it. To be frank, though, the lesson remains to be
learned by many firms. Youthful energy and exuberance lead
some to think they can do anything, if they just work hard
enough. My research and experience suggest that many Valley companies continue to have far too many initiatives on
their plate relative to their capabilities and capacity to complete them. In striking contrast to the other two portfolio assessment criteria, which are strongly influenced by external
factors, providing the right capabilities and sufficient capacity is well within the control of the firm.

Here's a quick vignette to illustrate what happens when
you run out of capabilities and capacity. Have you ever arrived at Los Angeles International Airport (LAX) late at
night? If so, then you've experienced the beauty of the L.A.
freeway system, because at two o'clock in the morning you
can get from LAX to Universal City in a half hour or less. Trying the same drive at five o'clock on Friday afternoon,
though, could easily take four times as long. Why? The freeway didn't change; there are just too many cars using it.

Since the near-term capacity of concrete freeways is fixed,
when more cars use them simultaneously, traffic slows until it
reaches gridlock. The few short-term options include remov-
ing cars from the freeway via carpools, metering, or fewer
entrances. In the longer term, adding lanes is your only option, but construction will constrain current capacity even
more. Just as these dynamics govern what happens on the
road, they also govern how innovation flows through your
firm. When the demand for resources approaches capacity,
throughput and flexibility drop dramatically, eventually creating innovation gridlock.

Taking an innovation from concept to launch and meeting

customer quality, yield, and volume requirements every step along the way requires capable people. Since innovation is a pervasive process that touches nearly every group inside the firm, the weakest link determines overall effectiveness and speed. No matter how small a group's involvement, when the demand on it exceeds its supply, a bottleneck forms and work grinds to a halt. (The weak link could be a drafting assistant or a marketer as much as an engineer; my research shows that overloads most often occur in areas not traditionally chartered with primary innovation responsibility.) And shifting people from one top-priority project to another is not very different from changing lanes during rush hour: you may feel like you're taking action to optimize the situation, but the impact is negligible.

To make matters worse, current customer support often draws on the same resources that drive new innovation initiatives. Once a new product or service is complete, the people working on it move on to the next initiative; when they are called back to resolve a current customer problem, they do so at the expense of the next innovation. Leaders often overlook this factor when estimating the resources devoted to innovation. The error compounds what is already a marginal balance between supply and demand.

The problem has nothing to do with behavior; it is simple physics. Just as you wouldn't try to pour five gallons of paint into a one-gallon pail, you can't expect people to perform effectively when demand is three times resources. Without question, humans are more creative than freeways, and they are more capable of dramatic productivity improvements. When Silicon Valley firms bet their innovation efforts on a constant flow of miracles, however, they're acting like they're smoking marijuana—and, unlike President Clinton, they're inhaling. Asking people to be creative and "make it happen" doesn't overcome demand that exceeds supply by 200 to 300 percent.

How do the Valley firms that understand this problem address it? There are two basic approaches, both driven by the same underlying premise. You should load your innovation system to no more than 85 percent of its actual capacity. This ensures that innovation traffic flows faster and, over time, that more projects get finished. Don't be afraid your people will only work 85 percent of the time; the unloaded 15 percent provides a buffer to handle all of the interruptions and unforeseen complications that arise.

The first method is a top-down judgment call, usually driven by an experienced leader (often the CEO) who simply will not let the firm get ahead of itself. I've seen this call made by listing all the initiatives in priority order, then drawing a line that defers initiatives below the line until those above it are completed. The leader's experience dictates where to draw the line. This approach works best when there are less than twenty initiatives, the work for each is relatively discrete, and the leader has a rich understanding of both the tasks and capabilities required to succeed.

The second approach is more analytical, although it avoids tracking everyone's time in detail. It first classifies innovation initiatives into broad categories, determined by size and skill requirements, and then creates templates that summarize the resource and capability requirements for completing each type. In a simple situation, you might have two profiles, one for revolutionary initiatives and one for evolutionary efforts. In more complex environments, you need more categories to reflect the initiative mix accurately. For example, you might have separate categories for hardware and software changes, or for partnered efforts versus internal ones. Usually, though, it's best to limit the total number of categories to less than six.

After the major categories are defined, the firm uses its past experience to define capability and capacity requirements for each category. Think of the result as a template for each class of initiative that describes the skill and level of experience of the people required, how many, and when. While this approach is not precise, it is far more effective than trying to track actual time allocations. Once you have the templates for each initiative type, it's a simple matter to compare the aggregate resource requirements over time to your total available hours.

Striving for more precision does not improve the value of this approach. It is very useful for assessing overall capacity, based on initiative mix, but it's not a substitute for project resource planning. Valley companies are filled with engineers who continually seek to manage work with the same precision they bring to engineering problems, but their attempts are often counterproductive.

Typically, only a few functions (such as engineering and manufacturing) track how much time and resource capability is required to execute each type of initiative; others will only have anecdotal information. By iterating and testing the templates as they are created with those who provide the information, you can quickly get to a point of reasonable accuracy. When Cirrus Logic's graphics company used this approach, they quickly saw how overloaded they were, as well as how they could leverage their existing skills by using common technologies across products.

That takes us to the next and more critical problem: getting people to address the overcapacity problem once they recognize it. This is a tough problem, since no one likes to defer a project, yet there are some things that help. First, always underscore that initiatives are simply being sequenced, not completely eliminated. If you get rid of innovation gridlock, it's likely that you can complete the deferred initiatives more quickly than if you continued the defective process. Second, if you can concurrently increase critical capacities or fix major process problems, you can often achieve a disproportional capacity improvement very quickly. For example, when Quantum changed its product architecture and went from three firmware architectures to one, it dramatically lowered the need for firmware engineers, thereby relieving what had been a longstanding bottleneck. Third, sometimes you can shift resources from one area to another, *if* the people have the necessary skills.

Capabilities and capacity take a long time to recruit and

develop. Remember that Silicon Valley firms have permeable boundaries, and they often extend both their human and technical capabilities by partnering with others. The time to establish these plans is when you're creating the innovation portfolio. If you wait until the teams working on the initiatives begin to scream, you're in rush-hour gridlock. As with freeway traffic, the best way to cope with gridlock is to prevent it in the first place.

Leverage and Risk

Disk drives are one of the most amazingly complex commodities in the Valley today. The recording head literally flies on a cushion of air, a scant few thousands of an inch above a disk spinning at 5,400 rpm. If you were to equate this to flying an airplane, you'd have to travel at nearly the speed of sound, hugging the ground at an altitude equal to the thickness of one sheet of this paper! Since the technology was created by IBM in the 1970s, disk-drive capacity has exploded while size has shrunk dramatically. For less than two hundred dollars, you can buy a disk drive that fits in your PC and has more than twenty times the capacity of the early drives that IBM mainframes relied upon.

In the early 1980s, Finis Conner started a new disk-drive company, Conner Peripherals, that eventually eclipsed Compaq as the fastest-growing company in U.S. history. Conner soon became an archrival to Quantum Corporation. This continuation of the Quantum-Conner story illustrates how Quantum also used leverage to mitigate its development and market risk, eventually catching and passing Conner, in addition to the organizational changes described earlier.

In 1989, while Conner was surging, Quantum was struggling. Apple was the latter's only major customer, plus the firm was late converting its products to the new 3.5-inch standard. An ill-fated manufacturing facility in Puerto Rico had been shut down, replaced by a strategic partnership with

Matsushita's MKE subsidiary. There were leadership changes as well.

By 1994, both Conner and Quantum grew to more than $2 billion in annual revenue (see Figure 4–5). Conner continued to lead the industry in the introduction of new form factors, being the first to bring the 2.5-inch drive to market and unleashing the portable computer market as we know it. During this period, though, Quantum not only grew faster but eventually surpassed Conner. In 1995 Conner was bought by Seagate Technology; it no longer exists. What happened?

During a strategy session in late 1988, Quantum leaders studied Conner's success, albeit with some defensiveness. Customers openly acknowledged that Quantum products were superior in quality, if not performance; at the same time, these products were rarely first to market. In the fast-moving heyday of personal computers, having the latest and greatest technology was often more important to PC manufacturers than quality. Customers had a tolerance for some quality problems if it enabled them to have the newest computer available.

One of the differences Quantum executives noticed was the architecture of their products versus those of Conner. If you looked at the circuit boards on the back of any Conner drive,

FIGURE 4–5

Quantum Versus Conner Revenues

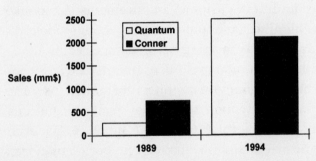

they looked essentially the same. In other words, Conner was getting leverage from board designs and components across all their products. In contrast, the circuit boards on each of the Quantum product lines looked completely different. If you opened the cover of each Quantum drive, you could see why—the servo mechanism that moved the recording head across the disk surface was different on each drive. Quantum used three different servo methods, each requiring its own chips, mechanics, firmware, and more. Conner used one servo design across all of its products.

The picture became clear to Quantum. Conner had developed what Wheelwright and Clark call a platform product: a core product design that can be tailored with small changes to meet many different customer applications.[4] In contrast, Quantum's designs were one-offs; each design was unique and independent. Quantum had to have engineers who were specialized in each servo method, marketing people had to learn how to explain all three methods to customers (and why there were three!), manufacturing required different test programs and part numbers for each method, and so on. Quantum responded to the problem by deciding to create platforms of its own, using a common architecture that could extend across its entire product line. They also designed a migration path to transition from the current architecture to the new platforms with the least amount of disruption.

When designing its new platforms, Quantum paid attention to embedding "hooks" from which it could easily create customized products. This required looking forward and making assumptions about future customer requirements. A modular design process allowed Quantum to create enough hooks for easy customization while meeting performance requirements and maintaining its common architecture. Between 1989 and 1994 it refreshed its common architecture platforms regularly, always paying attention to the performance and customization hooks. As Figures 4–6 and 4–7 illustrate, Quantum was able to leverage a slightly smaller number of platforms into five times as many derivatives. Paradoxically, while

FIGURE 4–6

Quantum Versus Conner: New Products

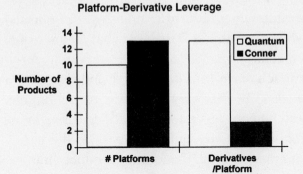

Platform-Derivative Leverage

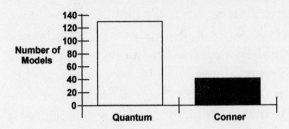

Total New Product Models, 1989–1994

FIGURE 4–7

Quantum Versus Conner: Productivity

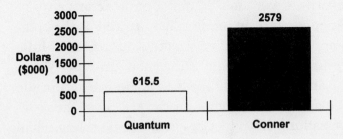

R&D Expenditures per Product, 1989–94

Quantum improved, Conner deteriorated; they began to develop products with the complexity of new platforms but failed to spawn many derivatives from them.

To put a capstone on this story, Quantum didn't achieve its

success by having more resources than Conner, nor by having brighter people. By working smarter in the fuzzy front end via thoughtfully designed product and process architecture, though, Quantum generated three times as many products as Conner while spending a fourth of what Conner did per product.

Quantum's approach also dramatically reduced risk for itself and its customers. Internally, by migrating to a common platform, it was able to concentrate employees' learning on a single product architecture. This quickly expanded the number of people who understood the entire product line in depth, because now everyone in manufacturing, test design, engineering, marketing, and sales worked on the same basic product. This in turn created more flexibility, since there were now several people who could respond to any problem. The platform approach also reduced the number of suppliers that Quantum relied upon, increasing its cost leverage; the same parts were used three times as much. Having fewer discrete products also reduced the amount of raw material inventory the company had to maintain, as well as all the expertise required to ensure high levels of incoming quality. Overall, the platform strategy simplified everyone's life at Quantum.

From the perspective of customers like Apple (and later Hewlett-Packard), Quantum's common architecture also increased their confidence in the product, as well as the company. Now, once Apple qualified a platform, it needed little additional testing to qualify any of that platform's derivative products. Thus the same simplification that occurred inside Quantum also occurred among its customers. Since the products across Quantum's product line were similar, Apple had the confidence to move Quantum products into new applications on its own. The platform strategy also meant that when Quantum undertook a new derivative, the degree of change was sufficiently small that it also confined risk and increased reliability. Thus Quantum was able to customize its products for Apple and Hewlett-Packard while simultaneously increasing the reliability and number of products it sold.

The same approach can also be seen in service companies. Mortgage banking thrives on platforms. The adjustable rate mortgage started as a breakthrough during the double-digit interest rates of President Carter's era and continues as a platform today, spawning extensions via small tweaks to terms and conditions. Likewise, the universal credit card is a platform that Visa and Mastercard have joyfully milked through such variants as airline mileage cards and debit cards.

Since services are easily copied, derivatives (or line extensions) are particularly common. For example, American Express offers certain corporate card services to small businesses that it doesn't extend to large accounts. In service, continually coming up with new line extensions that exploit a niche may be a better investment than a new platform. Introducing a sausage Egg McMuffin once you've established a bacon-only version is much easier than launching a new food (such as pizza) that requires additional equipment and training, in addition to greater market risk.

Leverage is what separates winners and losers. Although measuring the amount of money (as a percentage of sales) that a firm spends on innovation is very popular, there is little correlation between dollars spent and return. Containing risk while simultaneously creating leverage is the third assessment criteria for any portfolio. Let's now put our learning into action as we watch NetDrive, Inc. create its innovation portfolio.

NETDRIVE CREATES ITS INNOVATION PORTFOLIO

NetDrive, Inc., is a fictitious company that represents an amalgamation of Silicon Valley innovation experience. In addition to manufacturing data storage systems, NetDrive runs a data management service business targeted at large World Wide Web sites and companies with large internal intranets.

NetDrive provides real-time support to the these sites with a focus on security, data backup, and archival storage.

NetDrive Builds Its Portfolio

Like many Valley companies, NetDrive leaders assigned the preparation for their quarterly portfolio review to marketing with the expectation that the department would lead a multi-functional effort, minimally involving key technology groups, customer service, operations, and sales. To support this effort, Dave Black and Sheila Stone, NetDrive's CEO and vice president of marketing, met with staffers a month ago to define what they wanted to review at the meeting, and to provide oversight during the preparation process.

This quarter, Dave and Sheila asked for (1) a map of the current set of released products and services, by market segment, including key transitions and end-of-life targets; (2) a product/service roadmap that defined the next two generations of innovation initiatives; (3) a technology roadmap that defined core technology developments, as well as their timing and current status; (4) a brief update on the competitive environment, including trends within the customer, competition, and technology arenas; and (5) for each new proposed initiative, a one-page assessment that describes the initiative's value proposition, competitive product, return, investment required, risks and timing. Since NetDrive has been holding quarterly portfolio reviews for some time, what might seem like an enormous amount of preparation actually consisted only of consolidating and organizing existing information. Like most Valley companies, the focus was succinct answers, not mountains of paper.

Tom Swift, the lead member of the preparation team, kicked off the meeting with the competitive update. Tom covered trends in several domains, including customers, technology, competition, markets/channels, and global factors. As the executives listened to each trend in Tom's update, they modified or added implications to those listed by the prep

FIGURE 4–8

Environmental Scan Example

Domain	Trends	Implication
Customers	• Value segment increasingly important	• Cost sensitivity bleeding into office segment
	• Consolidation continues everywhere	• Relationships with future winners key—do we serve them?
	• Premium fragmentation	• Pick technology drivers in premium segment
	• Remote backup gaining acceptance	• Stress and expand SafetyNet™ across markets

team. Figure 4–8 provides a snapshot of some of the customer trends that were raised, along with their implications.

Having used this approach for more than a year, NetDrive executives have learned how to make the update quick and useful. First, they focus most of their attention on customer trends. (In NetDrive's early days, Dave Black used to preach a common Silicon Valley aphorism: know your customer, ignore your competition. While Dave has since mellowed, Net-Drive executives have not forgotten, and they are very wary of reacting too strongly to competitive developments.) Second, they never talk about trends without identifying implications for the innovation portfolio. Third, they know that not every trend requires a response. Fourth, they never end the update without creating a short list of key implications (five or fewer) that they use to test the portfolio.

Next, to establish a context for considering the planned in-

FIGURE 4–9

Product Roadmap

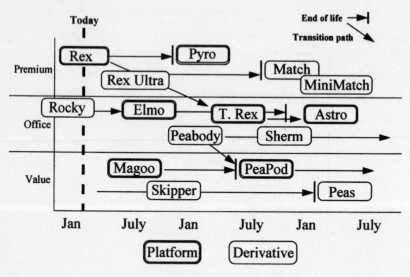

novation initiatives, Tom rapidly reviewed a map of current products and services. After a quick discussion of current business, Tom turned to the innovation portfolio, starting with the new products. On the first map he showed the new products, indicating platforms and derivatives by market segment. Also on this map was a new migration plan that his team was suggesting (see Figure 4–9). Tom's proposal was to leverage first-generation platforms, such as Rex, into second-generation products (T. Rex) in the market segment immediately below where the original was introduced. The intent was to increase technology reuse, thereby reducing cost and improving reliability. This idea stirred up a lot of discussion as executives debated whether this was feasible.

Although the executives liked the migration leverage, the key question was, how would they actually capture it? Some were concerned that by the time the original platform was altered to meet the needs of the new segment, NetDrive might be better off just designing a platform from scratch. To help with the discussion, Tom presented a second map using

FIGURE 4–10

Product/Process Matrix

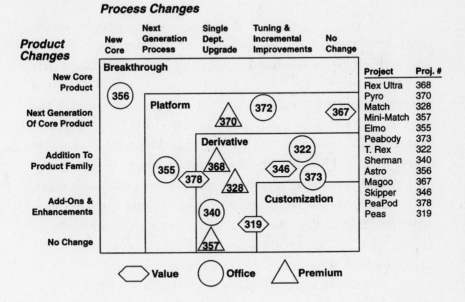

Wheelwright and Clark's product process matrix.[5] This map (see Figure 4–10) identified the new products as breakthroughs, platforms, derivatives, and customizations. The intent of the map was to illustrate the portfolio's stretch and resource requirements, since the size of each icon corresponded to the resource requirements.

NetDrive executives spent an hour discussing the migration suggestion. As valuable as leverage can be, Dave Black pointed out that when markets and technology are moving rapidly, a platform's ability to support a second generation of derivatives is questionable. To make his point, Dave cited the contrasting strategies of Silicon Graphics and Black & Decker.

Dave pointed out that unlike the PC business, which advances to a rhythmic beat set by Intel and Microsoft, the workstation business is a free-for-all based on who can extract the best price-performance combination. SGI's strategy is to dominate through unbeatable performance. Since reusing existing technology could constrain SGI developers from stretching for technologies that are at the forefront of performance, they are usually willing to give up the cost advantage of reuse, hoping to make it up by their performance edge.

Dave contrasted SGI with Black & Decker's success in the far more stable hand-tool industry. Black & Decker allocated $20 million to move from a product line that had thirty different motors, sixty different motor housings, and dozens of operating controls.[6] When it shifted to a platform model, the results were dramatic: product costs dropped by 50 percent, market share rose from 20 percent to a dominant share, and competitors declined from more than twenty to three. Dave's bottom line was to use leverage wisely, since it cuts both ways.

Returning to the NetDrive portfolio, the big question centered on Peapod. Peapod was projected to transform Peabody, a derivative from the office segment, into a platform for the value market. Ultimately, the consensus was that this was asking too much, and it was decided that Tom's team should re-scope Peapod as a new platform. They decided to experiment with the migration approach using T. Rex (which would be spawned by Rex, a platform in the premium sector).

Before closing the leverage conversation, Dave Black expressed some uneasiness about Astro as the only breakthrough product on the map. To alleviate his concerns, Mark Jackson, head of development, reviewed the technology roadmap. Mark had several initiatives on the technology map that, as yet, hadn't been linked to specific products. Temporarily satisfied, Dave asked Tom and Mark to make sure the linkages were defined and discussed at the next quarterly review.

Many of the questions that came up during NetDrive's deliberations provide a cogent summary that you can use to build and assess your firm's portfolio:

Stretch and Fit
1. Does the cumulative return of all initiatives meet our goals, including nonfinancial returns?
2. Are there any initiatives below expectations, and why?
3. Have we enough stretch in the mix of initiatives (break-

through, platform, and derivative) and within each initiative?

4. Does the strategy implied by portfolio match what we've defined?
5. Will this portfolio enable us to meet market share and growth goals in three years?
6. Do the portfolio and individual products meet customer windows? Where is it really tight?

Capabilities and Capacity

7. What are the resource requirements embedded in these recommendations? Where are our bottlenecks: real and potential?
8. What will this portfolio do to reduce the need for hiring more customer support people?
9. What's your confidence in the timing shown?
10. Where do our partnerships help? hurt?
11. Does the staging of the various introductions enable fast global launches?
12. Is there any invention that we're dependent upon to execute these new initiatives?
13. Are we constantly improving the time it takes to complete initiatives?

Leverage and Risk

14. What are the major risks for the portfolio? How are we addressing them?
15. Does the product and service portfolio match the content and timing of the technology roadmap?
16. Are there products outside each market's "sweet spot," and why?
17. Are we leveraging our suppliers as co-developers, particularly on platforms?
18. Where do we have one-offs, and why?
19. How would this portfolio compare, *in the customer's eyes,* to the competition? Where is it weaker and stronger?
20. Where are we trying to use leverage, and where have we chosen to forgo it?

The total discussions lasted for a good three hours and resulted in several significant adjustments. The NetDrive leaders then turned to the company's portfolio of service initiatives.

The Service Difference at NetDrive

The service portfolio was not controversial, but the large information technology investment that was required to support it created a lot of controversy. Frustrated, Dayton Duncan, general manager of NetDrive's service business, recalled that he frequently felt like a salmon swimming upstream at NetDrive, because his peers came from a product world and didn't understand the service development and delivery requirements. For example, the storage system business could build inventory ahead of time to meet unanticipated surges in demand. Data management services, though, were impossible to inventory. Data management had to be in place beforehand, since service creation and delivery happen at the same time. Similarly, if there are problems, Dayton noted, you can't recall a poor service as you can a defective storage system. Quality control and customer satisfaction all happen in the same instant. To provide reliable, defect-free service, the information technology investment was critical.

Dayton emphasized the difference by acknowledging that steps in service innovation followed the same basic path as product innovation, but with some significant twists. While the need to manage service innovation using a portfolio was the same as for product innovation, services are usually quicker to create and modify. For example, changing the terms of a service agreement is relatively easy compared to changing the performance of a data storage system. Additionally, the value NetDrive's customer received from data management services was hard to separate from the people delivering the service. Who assembled a storage system hardly mattered, but NetDrive's data management service representatives were the service in the customer's eyes. To compete, they had to have the right information available at all times.

Finally, Dayton argued that the information technology was essential to respond rapidly to competitive threats. In contrast to NetDrive's storage system technology, data management services could be easily copied by a competitor, and vice versa. The service business depends on a steady stream of quick-response derivatives and customizations to match competitive thrusts, special needs, and emerging customer trends. For example, when a competitor changed its data management rate structures, NetDrive sometimes had to respond almost instantly. Therefore, NetDrive's service portfolio usually defined primary service categories with the expectation that not every derivative would be listed. Many derivatives were created on the spot, as customers requested them. Dayton argued that this was the essence of service.

Making the Window

Before concluding, Black raised the credibility of the proposed timing, particularly within the product innovation portfolio. Anyone who had been at NetDrive for more than three years knew that meeting a scheduled introduction date was a rarity. A year ago, NetDrive had initiated a "fast cycle time" improvement effort, but it still suffered from having too many initiatives on the its innovation freeway. Black closed the meeting by asking Tom and his team to compare the portfolio against NetDrive's capabilities and capacity, and to alert him immediately to any problems that could affect those initiatives already under way.

SUMMARY

George Shultz, a former U.S. secretary of state, once commented that the only decisions he should make were those that *only* he could make. An insightful corollary to Jacques's decision theory, Shultz's comments apply to leaders during the early innovation phase. Only the firm's leaders can decide what directions to take, and what investments to make; they're the ones who can write the checks.

Much like Shultz's foreign policy world, innovation is full of unknowns and has access to fewer facts than daily operations. With the tools presented in this chapter, you certainly will make better choices, as well as have a better understanding of what is required to execute those choices successfully. Keep that radar scope turning and scanning, though, since your greatest successes will probably not be those you originally chose, but the ones you discover by serendipity along the way.

If so, you will be in some of the best company the Silicon Valley has to offer. Intel's second and richest incarnation began when Andy Grove and Bob Noyce decided to leave dynamic memory chips behind and reinvent Intel as a microprocessor company. When Netscape went public, Jim Clark became significantly wealthier than he did when his first company (Silicon Graphics) went public some ten years before. Sun Microsystems stalled for several years until the Internet and the Java software system pumped new energy into its veins.

5

The Relentless Approach
to Innovation

The last adjective I'd use to describe the typical Silicon Valley innovation process is *pretty*. Traditional aphorisms such as "If you can't define it, you can't design it" are violated daily, as projects lurch to a start without complete or stable definitions. It's not that people don't want a clear target; they'd kill for one. In the Valley, though, technologies and markets move so fast that what is possible changes daily.

Rather than having targets as sharply defined as a bull's-eye in a rifle range, Valley targets are like clouds on a breezy day. They change shape while moving, and just when you think that maybe they've stabilized, they shift again. With each breeze, some opportunities vanish, while others are unveiled—sometimes you suddenly see something, like the Internet, that wasn't there a moment before. The innovation process that succeeds in this environment is a relentless, opportunistic, and somewhat frenzied approach that pushes the leading edge of knowledge forward, one inch at a time. Like a swarm of bees, Silicon Valley innovators have uniquely learned how to define, design, and deliver innovation with a massive degree of flexibility and concurrency.

Valley relentlessness explains how Sun Microsystems created Java, a software system that became an Internet standard almost overnight. It started with a young engineer telling CEO Scott McNealy that he was going to leave and go to NeXT, where they were "doing things right." That incident eventually led to the creation of the Green Team, whose task was to create a computer for "normal" people. The Green Team found that current programming languages were fast, but they weren't reliable for consumer products. A new language, Oak, was created; it created a flurry of interest among customers, then faded quickly. After a few unsuccessful attempts were made to resuscitate Oak, the clouds shifted again, and the Internet appeared high and bright in the sky. Bill Joy, a founder and technical leader at Sun, saw the Internet potential in Oak. He came out of semi-retirement, called back some of the original Green Team, and turned Oak into Java.[1]

The Java story is a classic illustration of Valley opportunistic success, yet that same spirit ripples through less spectacular innovation efforts as well. In this chapter I'll explore the third element in our model, the innovation process. I'll start by quickly outlining the challenges that any innovation process must address, followed by an overview of the traditionally accepted methodologies. Then I'll return to the Valley to look at how companies there have wrung more effectiveness out of the traditional approach, and how many have replaced it with something far better. Finally, I'll take you twenty-five miles north to the city of San Francisco and show how a service firm, Charles R. Schwab, has invoked the Growth Attitude to create a world-class service innovation process.

THE INNOVATION PROCESS: AN OVERVIEW

Starting with getting to work each morning, everything we achieve is the outcome of some process, even if we walk through the steps unconsciously. Likewise, rapid innovation requires an effective innovation process. Not each step has to be followed with military precision, and even a good process will not compensate for inadequate capabilities or knowledge. Nor is there one innovation process that works for all companies, markets, technologies, or industries. The effectiveness of the process, though, is usually inversely proportional to the thickness of the notebook that describes it. The hallmarks of effective innovation in Silicon Valley include the following attributes:

1. It creates customer value through *complete* solutions.
2. It challenges the status quo, encouraging out-of-the-box thinking mixed with pragmatic business judgment.
3. It produces top quality at lightning speed.
4. It makes multifunctional involvement the path of least resistance.
5. It is responsive to change, but not so flexible that it accepts every request for change.
6. It spawns new knowledge about innovation, including reinventing the innovation process itself.
7. It is documented crisply via maps and charts, and implicitly communicated by words and practice.

Some Silicon Valley companies tell me their problem is that they don't have an innovation process. Not true. Although their process may not be documented and constantly varies, every firm uses some type of process. The dilemma is that most knowledge work processes are intangible. You can spot a person working on a specific task, but you can't see the entire innovation process until it's mapped. Particularly in younger Valley firms, the innovation process is part of the firm's tacit knowledge base, and therefore it is invisible.

For a young firm to grow substantially, though, it must eventually make the core elements explicit. When a firm lacks a publicly defined process, everyone operates based on their own past experience and assumptions. Because these are likely to be different, task timing, deliverables, and interfaces won't match up. As the firm grows, the differences and problems increase exponentially. This is why rapidly growing Valley companies often find it impossible to hold the pieces together, even when great individual work is accomplished. The amount of rework under such conditions is enormous.

Although high tech is becoming increasingly more complex, Silicon Valley firms generally shy away from large, elaborate innovation processes. If you're building a space shuttle, however, the process must have plenty of detail and controls. The same holds true for products or services with high potential liability, such as automobiles, pharmaceuticals, or air travel. Each of these efforts employs hundreds of people, for whom the process becomes the backbone of the effort. The circumstances are different, though, for twenty people creating a new battery charger or designing corporate Web sites or flower arrangements.

The Service Difference

Service companies are much more likely to lack a defined innovation process than manufacturing concerns. Why? Because defining and implementing service ideas is normally far less complex than it is with manufactured products. In the simplest of cases, you may need only the basic outline of a process; not using *any* defined process, however, becomes a bad habit. The limited research on service innovation suggests that one of the major causes of failure and inefficiency is the lack of a defined process. As you'll see when we visit Charles R. Schwab, with just a shade more discipline, service firms can significantly increase their innovation success rate and speed.

Gas to Solid

The process of innovation is not unlike the steps required to turn a gas into a solid. As you would with a gas, the first thing you must do is contain the idea by drawing some boundaries around it; then you have to apply pressure carefully to shape and transform it. This pressure includes ensuring that the idea meets customers' requirements, can be produced and delivered reliably, and will provides the financial returns you require. Just as some gases will explode when compressed, ideas and innovation can self-destruct if too much pressure is applied prematurely. At the same time, without enough pressure, ideas will drift and miss their mark. This is why loose-tight leadership is required. Throughout the innovation process you have to monitor conditions and make choices about when to squeeze or relax, usually with far less data than you'd like. That's both the art and the excitement of relentless innovation.

If there's a question that permeates the innovation process, it's how can we safely move forward? Is the market still there? Can we leap over the remaining technical hurdles? Can we deliver or manufacture it? Is the overall value proposition still valid and cost-effective? Should we continue to pour money into this if our competition isn't? Let's see what types of processes companies use to ask and answer these questions.

I'll outline four generations of basic innovation processes. Think of these as waves that hit the shores of different industries at different times. The first wave is the traditional phase-gate model, still in use but fading among Valley firms. The second wave is the modified phase-gate model, which came into being to address its predecessor's liabilities. Most Silicon Valley companies have relied on this. The third or "new wave" includes the first processes that seriously departed from the phase-gate approach. Led by innovation in the software industry, many Valley firms are increasingly employing this method. The fourth wave or "tsunami" reflects the very recent and enormous impact that occurs when innovation process meets the Web. Such top Valley firms as Silicon Graphics, Sun Microsystems, and Cisco Systems are at the leading edge of this approach.

THE FIRST WAVE: THE TRADITIONAL PHASE-GATE MODEL

Born in heavy manufacturing, the phase-gate approach is the oldest and by far the most common innovation paradigm in the world. It breaks innovation into a series of sequential phases, with gates that must be cleared before you can proceed to the next phase. Ideally, the criteria for passing through each gate and the person who decides whether the criteria have been met (commonly called the "gatekeeper") are clearly defined beforehand. The project progressively gains maturity, which is tested at each gate until completion. Driven by the need to reduce the risk of change when ordering expensive tools with long lead times, the phase-gate model's hallmark is an early "design freeze" that creates a stable target for the remainder of the innovation process.

Wheelwright and Clark describe the phase-gate model as a funnel with screens, where the mouth of the funnel represents the idea generation period.[2] Each screen has a clearly defined deliverable, as illustrated in Figure 5–1, that becomes the basis for deciding whether or how to proceed.

The gates provide a clear and distinct mechanism to ask and answer the question, should we continue? In Silicon Valley firms, gatekeepers are managers, usually one level above

FIGURE 5–1

Funnel and Gates

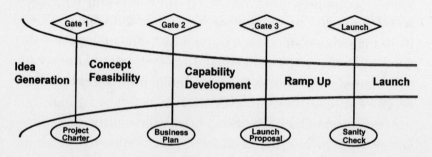

those working on the initiative. Outside the Valley, top executives often serve as gatekeepers so that they can control innovation cost and quality. In some Valley firms, the project team administers all or some of the gates using predetermined criteria.

The phase-gate model is effective under certain conditions. First, it works well when the time required to innovate is shorter than the rate of change in the business environment. For example, in the auto industry, the maturity of the technology, length of vehicle ownership, and high purchase cost make development cycles of 24 to 48 months acceptable. In contrast, Valley companies creating Internet software (such as Netscape) find that the market and technology change faster than they can innovate. In these situations, the phase-gate model is ineffective.

Second, the phase-gate model is very good at controlling quality and reliability. For a service business that needs ultra-high reliability (Federal Express, for example) the structured checkpoints of the phase-gate model are very effective. Similarly, although the individual technologies required for pharmaceuticals or aerospace—such as materials science—may move quickly, the tightly controlled process ensures regulatory compliance and product safety. You might get upset if Microsoft Word or Netscape's Web browser crashes when you're working; when a Boeing jetliner crashes, however, it's a problem of dramatically different proportions.

Third, the phase-gate paradigm is a good first step for companies that have never had a defined innovation process, wherever they may be. Just as you should get your manufacturing or service delivery process under control before trying to speed it up, the phase-gate approach stabilizes innovation. Once under control, you can adjust the number of phases and gates, as well as the rigor you apply to each.

That said, here are additional reasons that the phase-gate model is being challenged by alternative approaches:

1. *Low gatekeeper knowledge leads to poor judgments.* Gatekeepers, particularly when reviews are their only contact, rarely have sufficient knowledge to make good judgments.
2. *Slow and serial:* Concepts are rarely completely defined at the beginning, and the multiple "over the wall" transitions sap speed.
3. *Concept frozen too early.* The world changes and the hardest changes to deal with are those that occur after the concept is frozen.
4. *Focused on gates, not the customer.* People shift their attention from creating customer value to doing what's expedient to get through the next gate, since that is the more immediate problem.
5. *Review preparation time.* This step can become a tour de force of pretty presentations and dry runs, often in fear of management's gatekeeping authority.
6. *Narrow criteria.* Particularly with products, the criteria at the gate are often exclusively technical, with little market or manufacturing focus.
7. *Maturity focus versus learning focus:* Rather than setting a goal of learning as much and as fast as you can, gate requirements and timing establish a substitute target and rhythm.

The phase-gate model, in its religiously practiced form, is a holdover of the command and control paradigm. It doesn't harness the capabilities of today's knowledge workers or trust them to assess their progress honestly and adjust on their own. It has lost favor in the Silicon Valley because it doesn't fit with the shift from hardware- to software-intensive designs. Changing hard tooling at the last minute is guaranteed to be very expensive, but the ability to flip a bit of code the day before a product's release is something to take advantage of rather than guard against. Accordingly, many Valley companies have modified the phase-gate model to increase its flexibility.

THE SECOND WAVE: REMODELING
THE PHASE-GATE APPROACH

Under the pressures of today's competitive environment, the classical phase-gate rarely plays out the way it was designed. Many companies randomly adapt it, while some Silicon Valley firms are more deliberate in their modifications. The latter approach is preferred because it enables a common understanding across the team. Typical changes include the following:

1. *Don't require all initiatives to use it.* Breakthrough projects, those that are early in the process, and very simple derivatives can do fine without a formal process.
2. *Reduce the number of gates.* When the project exceeds predetermined boundaries between gates, Apple has its teams call an "out of bounds" review to insert a gate as required; otherwise, they flow freely.
3. *Making some gates optional.* Tailor the gates to the type of initiative (for instance, a derivative will have fewer gates than a platform effort), or depending on the amount and quality of progress
4. *Change gate criteria and gatekeepers.* Soften gate passage from an all-or-nothing proposition by allowing passage if most criteria are met (with recovery plans for the remainder), and make the team accountable for gatekeeping
5. *Limit gate review time and preparation.* Limit the number of slides, eliminate dry runs, and use predefined presentation formats.

Danger: When ISO Zealots "Fix" the Phase-Gate Model

Has your firm been "ISO'd"? I've seen excellent Valley innovation processes brought to a near standstill by overly zealous quality managers. If you work in service industries, you may not be as familiar with ISO 9000 (a quality standard that you must pass to sell goods and services in the European Economic Community, Common Market) as your counterparts in manufacturing. Like all quality programs, it's well-intentioned. Used properly (as it is by many Valley firms), all ISO 9000 requires is that you define and document the innovation process you'll use, then demonstrate that you in fact followed this process. The problem is that the quality function, like all others, has its share of diehards who sometimes confuse means and ends.

To ISO extremists, more stringent gatekeeping and documentation becomes an end unto itself. And when extremism is in the pursuit of quality, attacking it—especially in public—can be a career-limiting move. The solution is to stick with ISO's intent, using the gates to ensure customer value. With this focus, ISO 9000 can be quite helpful.

THE NEW WAVE: LESSONS FROM THE VALLEY

The phase-gate model is being increasingly challenged by the changes brought about by the global knowledge economy. You will see more of the following approaches in the years to come.

The Improv Model

Kathy Eisenhardt of Stanford's Engineering School argues that when the technical and business environment are both highly turbulent, formal processes such as the phase-gate approach are not nearly as effective as what she call the "improv" model, which uses a jazz combo as a metaphor. When jazz musicians come together, they create music through a process that's defined in real time, with a minimum of ground rules. There's always a formal leader who sets the tempo; the others look to him or her for cues about when they should get in or out. Eisenhardt's model comes from a study of more than fifty Silicon Valley companies' product development practices. She compared mature Valley firms, such as mainframe computer companies, with those from the more rapidly changing workstation industry.

The improv model works well when the unknowns are high *and* the players are seasoned. When inexperienced people work this way—just as when children first play music together—the result is not pleasing to the ear, or the balance sheet. The improv model doesn't discard structure, just as there is a clear structure to good jazz. Rather than having it overlaid from the outside, though, the improv approach builds structure from the inside as it is needed. That's why it requires a critical mass of experienced people to work.

The improv model is limited by three additional factors. First, it's not effective for very large projects; that's the equivalent of needing an orchestra but calling in a combo. Second, passing on the learning from one initiative to another is difficult, because much of the required tacit knowledge is woven tightly into the experience of those participating. Third, because the process is highly tacit, there's very little explicit knowledge available to teach others how to do it. It might be a reasonable way to learn jazz, but the risks and costs associated with innovation make it a significantly expensive business proposition. In short, this is not the first Silicon Valley technology I'd suggest importing into a non-Valley company.

Calendar-Paced Development and Prototyping

This approach is increasingly being used in the Silicon Valley, particularly in semiconductor companies. Rather than passing through gates after the initiative has reached required levels of maturity, programs are driven by calendar milestones. At each date, people gather around to review prototype or simulation results. Rather than testing it against fixed criteria, the team focuses on what is required to move the initiative forward.

The calendar-paced approach lends itself to customization for each initiative, and the connection to prototypes or simulations establishes a rhythm that hustles the initiative along. For example, in the phase-gate model, you can schedule when you'd like to go through the gate, but if you can't meet the gate criteria you have no choice but to wait. When this occurs, the focus invariably shifts from designing the overall project to getting through the gate. In the calendar model, the dates establish a pace for the entire project that can be modified by shifting the dates. As each date nears, people get ready to review the project, looking for what needs to be done to keep it moving. The reviews are focused on eliminating barriers and defining critical next steps. People pause to reflect and then get back to work relatively quickly, with a clear set of coordinated objectives. In effect, the gate or gatekeeper is replaced by a programmed pause for reflection, after which work continues.

The distinctions between the phase-gate and calendar models are threefold. First, the calendar model focuses on learning: what's occurred and finished, compared to what's still unknown. Second, the dates set a predictable rhythm, whereas the time between traditional gates may vary greatly from phase to phase. Third, the calendar model is more responsive to environmental changes.

Flexible Model

In a nutshell, Silicon Graphics' business strategy is to always be the performance leader. SGI hates to lock down any decision earlier than absolutely necessary for fear it will miss a newly emerging technology. Tightly in sync with the Growth Attitude, this strategy is not served well by the traditional phase-gate model, with its bias toward locking on to a single concept in the early phases.

SGI's solution, as detailed and described by Marco Iansiti, violates the classic injunction of "define it before you design it."[3] What SGI does is overlap concept definition with development. As illustrated in Figure 5–2, this is different from what is called "concurrent engineering."[4] Concurrent engi-

FIGURE 5–2

Traditional Versus Flexible Development

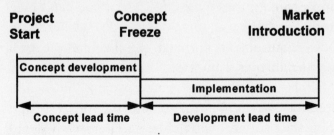

Traditional

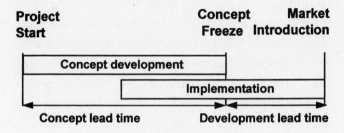

Flexible

neering refers to the parallel involvement of such functional resources as marketing, design, manufacturing, and service within each phase of the traditional phase-gate model. The flexible approach, which SGI uses, overlaps phases rather than functions.

You might look at the flexible model and think, "Hey, that looks like how we do it." Maybe so, but ask yourself if your firm stretches concept development intentionally, or only because of a loose implementation of the phase-gate approach. On paper, in fact, the flexible model doesn't look any different than a phase-gate approach with loose gatekeeping. The power in the flexible model is that the development process and tools are explicitly designed to support this overlap. In contrast, when the concept phase bleeds into development in the phase-gate model, it's unplanned and potentially troublesome. Iansiti quotes an SGI engineer as saying that the phase-gate model plants stakes in the ground during the early phases, and you're married to them for the rest of the project. In the SGI approach, for every stake planted, there's a way to pull it out.

What are the requirements to make the flexible approach work? The first enabler is a multidisciplinary core of highly experienced "architects." Seasoned veterans from hardware, software, product packaging, manufacturing process and even marketing are the ones who define and iteratively detail the overall architecture of the innovation. Using block diagrams, the innovation and its interfaces are described. The veterans' experience is essential to know what can be decided early versus what should wait until the last minute. It also provides the team with the strength to rip out a faulty concept element, and the composure to minimize the disruption. If you lack experienced architects, the flexible approach should be avoided.

The second enabler is the use of frequent prototyping and simulation. The latter is key in that SGI literally creates a software model of the entire product before it commits to hardware. This is a huge difference that requires the company to purchase and build the computational resources, as well as have the mindset to work this way. The advantage, though, is formidable. It creates what Iansiti describes as a "living specification" that enables rapid verification of the system-level impact of individual technical choices. If a new technology appears midway through the project, the model can be used to simulate its benefit.

The third enabler is Silicon Graphics' high level of vendor and customer inclusion. Through nondisclosure agreements, SGI seeks early development feedback from its "lighthouse" customers—the ones who push the technology the hardest, thereby shining a light on cutting-edge requirements. Similarly, because component vendors are considered the experts in their respective technologies, SGI defers to them and directly involves them in the project. Going beyond merely consulting (which is commonplace today), SGI engages its suppliers as full partners in the value definition and creation process, often co-locating them onsite.

Fourth, the flexible approach requires focus. If your innovation freeway is packed to gridlock with initiatives, don't even consider this approach. Shifting people (and particularly architects) from one project to another destroys the coherence required to manage flexible development.

THE TIDAL WAVE: WEB-BASED INNOVATION

The most exciting development in the Valley these days is the use of Web-based development. Led by Sun Microsystems, Silicon Graphics, and Cisco Systems, companies are making their internal Web sites (called *intranets*) the backbone for innovation. In Cisco's Core Products Group, the innovation programs are alive on the Web, including review documents. Review and weekly team meetings use actual Web pages (via a projector linked to the Web) so that people in other locations can follow along by conference call. Each team has its own home page, and technical documents and backup materials relating to any element are only a click away.

This is not just a Cisco phenomenon; Silicon Graphics has more than 600 internal Web sites and 100,000 pages of information available. Items ranging from inventory information to employee benefit forms are available on the Web. At Cirrus Logic, each innovation team has its own home page, with an electronic dashboard that provides a quick and comprehensive update on its projects.

What's Behind the Tidal Wave?

Why is there so much excitement in the Silicon Valley about using the Web for innovation? First, it broadens the velocity and distribution of information even more than e-mail. E-mail depends on the sender's thoughtfulness to touch everyone. In contrast, having a home page for each project enables anyone to drop in at their own convenience and rummage through the entire program via hot links. For example, if you're in a support role that requires you to work with several initiatives, it's impossible to attend all of the meetings and still get your work done. This creates a dilemma: since you don't really know what's going on, you don't know what questions to ask or who should answer them. With an intranet, people in sales, field service, or logistics can rapidly access the information they need from each initiative *and* provide input as well. Intranets make tacit processes within departments visible to those outside. Multifunctional and cross-hierarchy involvement blossoms via the Web.

Second, as innovation becomes increasingly global, the Web provides a hub that enables round-the-clock access to information. You don't have to wait for an e-mail or voice mail message to be returned. Plus, with the Web's ability to carry sound and video, it's possible to share tacit as well as explicit data. Focus group videos can be downloaded and viewed locally instead of written reports based on one person's interpretation.

Third, reporting hierarchies become increasingly unnecessary once people can gather information and interact on their own. One of the great powers of the Web is to disintermediate distribution channels. Inside the organization, this has often been a role for management. With the Web, however, more management is done by the people themselves. For example, in my own consulting practice, we use Lotus Notes to create "team rooms" for each case. By wandering through the ongoing dialogue and client presentations housed within each team room, you quickly develop a rich understanding of what's going on. People working on similar cases can browse and see if there's something in another one that would be useful to them. In addition, we maintain a "knowledge bank" where nuggets of wisdom from all cases are stored to leverage and bridge learning from case to case.

Fourth, there are some simple technical features that make the Web a powerful tool. For example, putting something away and finding it later is much easier on the Web than with paper filing. Rather than each person having his or her own filing cabinet, everyone uses the same one. Today's search engines can retrieve a "lost" Web page and documentation much faster than you or I can look around someone else's cubicle for that critical piece of paper. You don't even need to know the report's title or date; if properly indexed, a search engine can find something by looking for a single word, such as an attendee's name.

The Web also uses the existing computer infrastructure in your firm. All you need is a Web server and browsers for each user. Many firms have a mix of new and old systems that can't talk to each other; it's frequently impossible to transfer data or even send e-mail from one system to another. Intranets cut through all this because they operate across platforms. The bottom line is that the absolute cost of an intranet is low, and the value-to-cost ratio is extraordinarily high.

How the Intranet Changed Customer Service at Cisco Systems

Let's bring Web-based development to life with a brief example. Cisco's growth has been phenomenal—yet with each router, hub, and switch sold, the support requirement also grows. It quickly became clear to CEO John Chambers that unless something was done to decouple support growth from the installed base of products sold, the support organization would grow to unmanageable proportions. He challenged the support group to maintain customer satisfaction while flattening the growth in head count. They accepted the challenge and moved some of their support services to an intranet. Since Cisco's customer satisfaction survey is also the centerpiece of compensation, people were rightly nervous that the Web might be negatively perceived by customers as a high-tech but low-touch solution.

In implementing their approach, the support staff decided to place all known bugs and software fixes on the service Web site. Clearly bugs outnumbered fixes, but they chose to be open and take the pressure. External customers were given access levels based on their service contract provisions; Cisco also provided query forms for support requests. Surveys after the switch to the Web showed that customer satisfaction with service—formerly provided exclusively by phone—has increased!

But that doesn't tell the whole story. Cisco employees can also access the service site (as well as other functions' home pages) to see how their division's products and services are performing. Rather than having to rely on what some unseen person defines as important enough to pass on, anyone can quickly get a snapshot of current problems. Conversely, the customer service staff can check the home pages of innovation teams to make sure their issues are being addressed in the next generation products. The time needed to detect a problem is usually longer than the time needed to correct it; the Web dramatically shortens the time to detect.

Valley Pragmatism: Tips to Stay Flexible

Swarming. Competing in an environment where startups nip at the heels of established companies and market windows slam shut in the blink of an eye requires an innovation process that's fast, flexible, and effective. Since the amount of change that occurs during the average development period is high, you can bet that innovation won't proceed exactly as it's described.

In the Valley's smaller companies, often the only written description you'll find is a project schedule; the intensity of human interaction compensates for the inevitable technical and communication glitches. Startups are particularly skilled at swarming around a single initiative with blinding focus. The development process is driven by the experience in the room, as well as the pressure to succeed. It's the improv model in action, because no startup begins with a formal development process. This is how Polycom created its ubiquitous star-shaped, gray conference phone (which you've probably seen in meeting rooms).

Larger companies usually have defined and documented innovation processes. The real question, though, is how much these represent what actually occurs. In practice, the defined process appropriately serves as a template, from which teams divert and swarm, based on their experience and the needs of their project. By and large, the older and larger the company, the more likely it is that the process is both out of date and out of practice.

In contrast to many other industries, Silicon Valley companies spend relatively little time conducting financial analysis. Once the market is confirmed and a few gross margin assumptions established, financial thinking nearly disappears. Development budgets such as you find in Detroit are rare. The focus is on hitting the window—because if you miss it, there will be no revenue.

Minimalist financial analysis. Visitors to Silicon Valley companies are frequently surprised that the ratio of financial people to total employees is much lower than in most industries. It makes sense and is something that you should question in your own innovation process. Far too much time is spent calculating estimated revenue, market share, and costs too early in development, when the data are poor and the concept is still quite fuzzy. After establishing financial boundary conditions, avoid distracting people from defining and designing.

Definer-designers. Valley development teams are often initially led by a technical person. Cirrus Logic CEO Mike Hackworth calls these people "definer-designers." The definer-designer travels to customers with marketing; during these visits, he or she has the technical ability to offer and explore choices that inquire into the assumptions buried behind customers' declared needs. The definer-designer may also offer alternatives that employ technologies about which the customer is unaware. Most marketing people don't have the technical background or currency to do this.

Active executive interest. Unlike their counterparts in many industries, senior Valley executives take an active interest in innovation. Frequently they serve as sponsors of major innovation teams, and they'll get deeply involved when an initiative ventures out of bounds. They often play a leadership role in the management of partner and supplier relationships. Compared to other geographies, including the technology belt along Boston's Route 128, Valley executives are biased toward an "open kimono" approach in sharing information with their partners and suppliers. A steady supply of current information is essential to making the large numbers of partnerships work. In fact, feedback from suppliers is often a critical indicator of a Silicon Valley firm's development effectiveness.

SERVICE INNOVATION: GROWING THROUGH INNOVATION AT CHARLES R. SCHWAB

It may sound like an oxymoron, but there *is* product development in service, and there's no better place to see it in action than at Charles R. Schwab. While best known for its low-cost consumer operation, Schwab has developed a large business serving professional financial advisors. This Financial Advisory Service (FAS) has grown from 100 employees in 1990 to more than 1,200 in 1996, with a base of 5,000 customers. Schwab measures growth by looking at the assets managed for customers, and it maintains growth targets of 20 percent or greater. New services play a huge role in how it increases these assets and its market share, and FAS has been a major contributor.

Collectively, money managers represent a large dollar volume of trading, but they are a highly fragmented market; one money manager may have fewer than twenty clients. It used to be that every time a money manager made a trade, he or she had to place a separate order for each customer, even if five customers were buying the same security. He or she also received separate trade confirmations for each customer. In short, it was a paperwork nightmare.

When FAS started, it had a tough time getting the attention of the organization. Schwab was functionally organized, plus FAS was quite small. Developing a new service required a sequential tossing of ideas over the wall between FAS and the core operations group. Eventually, FAS became so frustrated that it outsourced new service development. Schwab saw this happening and realized that in its business, information technology (IT) *is* the service "factory," and outsourcing was not a viable long-term option. The IT function since has been moved into the business units, who manage their own development.

In contrast to product innovation, service innovation usually is quite quick. At FAS, a small innovation takes less than three months, with most finished in less than six months. The overall process mimics a modified calendar-based model. Each project has established milestones for reviews, where it can be canceled if the market has moved or the project is not progressing.

The process begins with annual budgeting (humorously referred to as the "annual budget crisis"). Here, asset growth innovations and a few cost-reduction projects vie for funding. Most innovation descriptions are high level with minimal financial data, much like those in the Silicon Valley. Schwab has several customer advisory boards that participate in the definition of new innovations via annual meetings in San Francisco. As in the Valley, senior management is actively involved, but as informal partners. Elaborate presentations are frowned upon.

Once launched, projects use a high degree of prototyping that is similar to the calendar approach described earlier. Milestone assessments are both quantitative and qualitative, but the qualitative analyses are more important. Customer and senior management input helps the group developing the innovation look "outside the box" for nuances that hit the customer-value target squarely. Schwab also launches innovations into the market quickly without trying to get them perfect, adapting feedback from early users to tune the innovation for success. The results speak for themselves: of the 5,000 FAS customers, 75 percent are active users of the Schwab Link system.

The Dilemmas of Service Innovation

The Schwab case represents the leading edge of service development. Far more frequently, innovation is an ad hoc process, with success determined by the persistence and position of whoever has the idea. If you're high enough in an organization, force of position alone can help you corral the required resources to drive your idea home. If you're not, though, most service firms don't have a defined process for collecting, sorting, and driving innovations. There are a few (such as Nuveen) that have defined champions for innovation, and a process that is essentially based on what was done the last time.

The innovation processes used by manufacturing companies might be overkill, yet the ad hoc approach used by most service companies is not the right answer either. First, when there is not a defined service innovation process, innovation is purely a function of the employee or a manager seeing its value. If neither one pushes the effort, it rarely gets further exposure. Second, without a process, the chances for success are also dependent on how much cooperation can be begged, borrowed, or stolen. Third, the effort that is expended—particularly if the champion is relatively low in the organization—is much larger than it needs to be. Fourth, the chances of any individual getting the timely cross-functional commitment required to turns ideas into reality are not high. Remember, innovation is an interruption to today's operations issues, to which most personal goals and objectives are linked. The need to get attention to a new idea without a defined process makes an already difficult road even harder to travel. Finally, any big idea probably also requires a large investment; without a defined process, it is going to have a very difficult time being heard.

The answer is not to replicate what occurs in manufacturing companies, but rather to take a model such as the flexible or intranet-based approach and tailor it to service. Keep the speed and flexibility that is required to get to the market quickly, and use real market feedback instead of depending on market research.

Summary

If you only focused on the continuous flow of new products and services from the Silicon Valley, you would miss its primary contribution: a new approach to innovation. This attitude provides the essential glue, since any of the described approaches will undoubtedly hit some serious potholes along the way. Though each of the approaches varies in the amount of regimentation, none of them are undisciplined. It is the discipline of relentlessly driving to create something new that sustains Silicon Valley as the innovation capital of the world.

In the coming years, we will see further changes as the software content and intelligence imbedded in all products and services continues to expand. The phase-gate model will undergo even more modifications, and there will be a wave of thinking that follows the enormous impact of Web-based innovation processes. Without question, we will see more use of disciplined innovation processes within the service sector, tailored to their specific needs and competitive conditions. Taking all these improvements for granted, though, the heart of innovation will always depend on people. They are the focus of the next chapter.

6

The Collective Power
of Passion

The spirit and passion of Silicon Valley is best seen at the extremes of the workday. Breakfasts at Hobie's, a chain of health food restaurants that populate the Valley, launch not only companies but many of the exciting innovations within them. Evenings start around 7:30 at the microbreweries and exercise clubs, where the discussions continue. "Flex time" really means that there's no time when people aren't willing to probe and test new opportunities. What might appear to outsiders as normal after-work chatter is often just a continuation of an important meeting in a new venue. Around nine, people scatter; some go home to read their day's e-mail, while others return to the office (because now's the best time to get thinking work done).

Just as work bleeds through into the evening, the norms of daily living penetrate the workplace. Most wear to work the clothes they'd wear if they were staying home. You'll see coats and ties more frequently among sales and marketing people, but that's a personal choice. Whereas many companies declare publicly that people should be treated with respect, the Valley doesn't dole out the amount of respect based on hierarchical position. Anyone can talk to anyone without prior approval, or without the accompaniment of one's boss. The only assigned parking places in the Valley are for visitors and handicapped. Should you walk into a meeting in one of the more confrontative cultures, such as Sun Microsystems or Intel, you could easily find a newly minted college graduate arguing vehemently—and productively—with a senior executive.

The organization structures that these people work within are best described as flexible, permeable, and fluid. Reorganization is a way of life in the Silicon Valley. Organizations mimic nature's most adaptive organisms as they constantly reformulate themselves to meet the latest challenge. In contrast to traditional firms, where organization structure defines the framework within which work occurs, Valley firms use the work to define the organization's structure. Ironically, though, this distinction would be invisible if you compared a traditional firm's organization chart to one from the Valley. In the latter case, the functional hierarchy may look the same on paper, but it has little relationship to how the company actually operates.

In this chapter I'll address the fourth element of the Innovation System, the role of people and organization. I'll begin with what is by far the most important element—people. What makes the Valley's knowledge workers tick? What gets them excited? How can you motivate them? How do you get past the functional myopia that rich expertise often spawns? What about those who are, in a word, difficult personalities? We'll address these questions and then turn to the organization structures they work within, all the while focusing on what facilitates innovation. To that end, Valley firms make very clear choices that we'll explore.

WHAT MAKES KNOWLEDGE WORKERS TICK?

One of the oldest characterizations of Silicon Valley is that people really don't work for individual firms such as Intel,

Quantum, Heartport, or Hewlett-Packard, even if they happen to park their cars there. With average turnover of 15 percent combined with a continuous flow of new startup opportunities, everyone really works for a virtual company: Silicon Valley Incorporated.

Skills are both so abundant and in such demand that most people could quickly contribute at several Valley firms. The inducements that companies have historically used to secure loyalty have lost their clout; compensation and benefit parity is essential to get people through the front door, but it won't be sufficient to retain them. The potential for wealth creation is certainly an additional attraction, but it also won't buy long-term loyalty. When stock prices stagnate or fall, the exercise price on options can fall below the market, quickly creating a demotivator. This is often true for those that join a firm shortly after its initial public offering. In the terms of Abraham Maslow's famous hierarchy of needs, most Valley employees are far beyond the basic survival and security issues that formerly bound people to companies in Henry Ford's era.

In response, Silicon Graphics' Ed McCracken argues that *all* employees ought to be viewed as consultants. McCracken's mindset is useful because it acknowledges that in knowledge work, the power often shifts from what the employee offers the firm to what the firm offers the employee. His perspective puts pressure on company leaders to generate a magnetism that attracts people to the opportunities, challenge, and growth they can achieve as both individuals and professionals.

Like all knowledge workers, Valley people want to be considered and treated as *professional partners*. As professionals, each has studied and internalized a body of knowledge and code of conduct that supersedes the company for whom he or she works. They require that you respect their expertise, support them in its application, and help them extend it further. As partners, they want influence in decisions that determine where and how their expertise is applied to specific innovation initiatives, as well as how it contributes to the overall business strategy. Treat them as though they were just a technical pair of hands, and they will turn into very unhappy (and, more importantly, unruly) campers.

Leading in this environment is challenging at best, and more frequently like herding cats! These workers have strong individual beliefs and personalities; they respond much better to being pulled than being pushed. They need to know *why* something is being asked of them, and they must also have an opportunity to digest, test, and challenge when necessary. Like other knowledge workers, Valley people respond best when you (1) respect their professional status and identity, (2) provide challenging work, and (3) minimize the management burden.

1. Professional Status and Identity

Peers and networking. Since Valley workers' primary identification is with their profession, they are much more sensitive to the kudos they receive from their peers than those they receive from management. Most of this response occurs through informal networking, inside as well as outside their own company. Networking helps them benchmark their personal efforts and assess how well their company keeps abreast of new technology and opportunities.

For these reasons, public praise, positions such as corporate "fellow" or "chief scientist" (as they have at Apple, SGI, and Quantum), and even peer review can be extremely powerful motivators. As a leader, you've got to work the peer network actively. For example, don't try to manage a difficult employee on your own; he or she is probably difficult for others as well. Reframing the problem from a boss-employee situation to a workgroup issue can be surprisingly effective. Get their peers involved, since letting them down often has a much faster and stronger impact on the employee than letting the boss down.

Keep current, keep happy. Knowledge depreciates far more rapidly than hard capital assets such as equipment. Within a rapidly changing environment, the latest information and knowledge is essential for sustained success. Some Silicon Valley people are nearly manic about staying on the leading edge; a colleague of mine describes this behavior as FMS ("Fraid of Missing Something") syndrome.[1]

FMS-induced anxiety is only relieved by a steady flow of information, complemented by a regular pulsing of peers and leaders to reassure themselves that the information they're receiving is the best of what's available. Those who have a high FMS quotient constantly test to make sure their company's innovation pace and focus is in step with industry leaders. The young engineer who told Sun Microsystems CEO Scott McNealy that he was going to NeXT because "they were doing things right" exemplifies the need Valley workers have to be on the leading edge.

Keeping current transcends company boundaries. A unique Valley norm that distinguishes it from other areas, including Boston's Route 128 community, is that when you are facing a really tough problem, you contact *anyone* who may help, regardless of where they work. Obviously, those who work for competitors may be less forthcoming, but you'd be surprised how frequently these conversations take place. In my executive role at Silicon Graphics, I frequently sought help from people at Sun Microsystems and Hewlett-Packard, both direct competitors. Long before the Internet became a household word, Valley engineers used it to explore technical issues with their peer networks as they shifted from one company to another. The bottom line is that an individual's effectiveness is based on results and credibility, perceived reputation, and network of relationships rather than formal authority, job description, or position in the hierarchy.[2]

Showcase professional contributions. Professional contributions, including publishing and presenting at industry conferences, are also important, particular for those employed in research. Genentech, the biotechnology powerhouse located just north of Silicon Valley, handles this issue well in an industry that traditionally is very closemouthed.

Historically, drug manufacturers discourage publication for competitive reasons, normally insisting on a one- to two-year delay. This effectively makes it impossible for any researcher to claim ownership for a breakthrough. In contrast, Genentech's patent attorneys scrutinize new discoveries within a week, then let the researchers reveal their findings to the world *without even waiting for the patent application to be filed.*

This approach has yielded extraordinary results. According to the *Science Watch* newsletter, Genentech ranked fourth among research institutions in molecular biology and genetics based on the number of citations per paper, beating out universities such as MIT, Princeton, and Harvard. CEO Kirk Raab says that Genentech's policy toward publication and independent research does more than help lure top minds—it drives them to do great work. "Money is the ultimate report card but not the incentive," says Raab. "What really drives highly educated knowledge workers is pride in accomplishment."[3]

The ultimate skin: gain sharing. From the very beginning, Silicon Valley has been a place where strong technical leaders, with a little luck, can become wealthy. Take the recent case of Marc Andreessen, the University of Illinois graduate student who created Mosaic, the first World Wide Web browser. He went from graduate-student poverty to being a multimillionaire a little less than a year after joining Silicon Graphics founder Jim Clark to start Netscape Communications. While Andreessen's story is extreme in terms of amount and speed, Valley companies use equity, phantom stock, and royalties as a way of sharing the wealth generated by new technologies.

A key difference between wealth creation in the Valley and in traditional firms is the absence of a predefined upper limit. Equity across compensation and stock options is monitored, but you'll also find examples of individuals and teams who are rewarded with an unlimited percentage of the profits from a particular product. The underlying philosophy is that if people get rich while the company gains, it's no problem. This practice is most common in smaller companies where the risk is greatest; older firms have options for senior management and discounted employee stock purchase plans for all.

Overall, the Valley's approach to gain sharing has five beneficial effects. First, it evokes the entrepreneurial spirit, which in turn heightens energy and pushes creativity. Second, it forces people to look beyond technology to the value that it creates for the customer. As sexy as a new technology may be, until it brings additional value to a large set of customers, the chances of raising the capital required to fund a business are slim. Third, having to understand the nontechnical requirements makes technical people better team players, because they realize that they cannot deliver customer value unless their efforts mesh with others'. Fourth, it makes them greedy. As a result, people won't waste their time on ideas that can't be commercialized. (On the negative side, personal assessments of a technology's value may be significantly higher than those of customers or investors.) Last, sharing the wealth eliminates the resentment, demotivation, and turnover that frequently occur when the technologist receives an engraved copy of his or her patent certificate while the "suits" get wealthy from stock options.

2. Providing Challenging Work

The challenge factor. The professionals' true calling is the quality of the work itself. There's nothing more powerful to Silicon Valley workers than going where no one has gone before. If they believe the challenge is meaningful and exciting, then no obstacle is so big that it can't be overcome. A positive work environment is certainly desired, but if forced to choose between challenging work in an average environment or mundane work in a terrific environment, most knowledge workers will gravitate to the challenging work.

Silicon Graphics uses this principle to its advantage. As the technology leaders in 3D visual computing, SGI keeps the challenge factor high by cultivating what CEO Ed McCracken calls lighthouse customers—the ones who push SGI engineers to the limit and then some. Walt Disney Imagineering Group, for example, designs new attractions for Disney's theme parks.[4] For years, it has wanted to create a virtual-reality ride where tourists would strap on special headgear that gave them the illusion of being in a movie (for example, flying on Aladdin's magic carpet) rather than watching it. Using older SGI systems, motion sometimes seemed jerky or subtly out of sync enough that it made viewers nauseous. The Disney people have asked for a graphics system that will recreate the look of the movie without any compromises. For a knowledge worker, challenges of this sort make going to work exciting.

Provide the best tools. Valley workers live by their tools. In large part, tools determine their overall efficiency and effectiveness. When hampered by substandard tools, Valley workers resent working longer and harder than they know they need to. It's not like the old assembly line, where people took whatever you gave them; knowledge workers know what's possible, and they can't be fooled. Their patience is particularly short when they are working on essential but low-value features. The work isn't attractive, and a poor tool set simply extends the agony.

No Silicon Valley company understands and acts on the importance of tools any better than Intel Corporation. Living on the cutting edge means that commercially available tools trail the leading technologies, usually by a generation or more. Knowing this, Intel invests heavily in tools, both purchased and internally developed. Between 1984 and 1989, Intel spent $250 million—about 20 percent of its entire research and development budget—fine-tuning its CAD tools. The commitment, though, paid off: during that time, Intel cut chip development time by more than half, to an average of forty-four weeks. The development cycle time for the 486 was shorter than for the 386, even though the newer chip was a lot more complicated.[5] Getting commitment from Valley workers to reduce cycle time is a lot easier when the company provides the latest tools available.

Keep the innovation process simple and flexible, with clear roles. When Valley workers perceive that the time and energy consumed managing the innovation process is equal to or greater than the time they have for the work itself, productivity plummets and frustration soars. It's a difficult problem even if the perception is not matched by reality.

For this reason, you're better off to stay away from elaborate documentation, such as fat binders that document each and every requirement of the process; a one-page map will do fine. Better yet, enlarge the map so it's big enough for everyone to see while they are seated at a conference table. Then hang it in the team's meeting room, along with defined decision roles. Keep meetings task-focused and short, with only the critical people present. When larger groups are required, make sure the deliverable required from the meeting is defined at the start, and don't stray from the topic.

Although Valley workers' technical capabilities are highly sophisticated, their skills for understanding group process or leadership are conversely low. Two factors make the problem difficult. First, group process and leadership skills require primarily tacit knowledge, whereas product and technology knowledge is explicit and easily documented. Second, Valley workers who pursued technical fields place a high value on explicit knowledge, and thus they may denigrate tacit group and leadership skills as "soft."

Match task and resource requirements. As I noted during the discussion of strategic alignment, putting more initiatives in play than you have the capacity to execute quickly demotivates Silicon Valley workers. They're turned on by stretch objectives, but not overwhelming ones. By far, this is the most common sin my colleagues and I find within (and outside) the Valley. As I also noted earlier, this underlines the interdependence between the elements in the Innovation System. If you nail the organization and people element but have a poor process, or a severely overloaded development freeway, the organization and people will quickly become unglued.

3. Minimizing Management Overhead

Use "swiss cheese" management instead of a hierarchy. Valley knowledge workers are not unique in their impatience with bureaucracy, too many meetings, or bosses that tell them too much of what they should do. These things violate their sense of professionalism. At the same time, most accept that you can't let everyone have their own way and still produce a compelling new product or service. Rather than focusing on who's in charge, as you would in a hierarchy, a far more effective approach is to define what work is required, identify the key interdependencies, and than parse the task to small, interlocking teams with defined leaders. I describe this approach as "Swiss cheese management"; Figure 6–1 shows how it works at Quantum.[6]

The holes in the cheese are innovation subtasks where teams work, complete with defined goals, schedule, and accountabilities. Once these parameters are specified and agreed to, functional management provides resources but stays out of each team's "hole" unless it is not meeting its major commitments.

The solid cheese that keeps all the holes together is management's space. Management crafts the firm's overall shape, provides capabilities, and links the non-adjacent holes as necessary. The underlying premise for this approach is that knowledge workers want freedom and responsibility in defined areas, not *all* areas. When there are no holes of accountability, then there's nothing the knowledge workers own, and it's pretty tough to care much about something you

FIGURE 6–1

Swiss Cheese Management

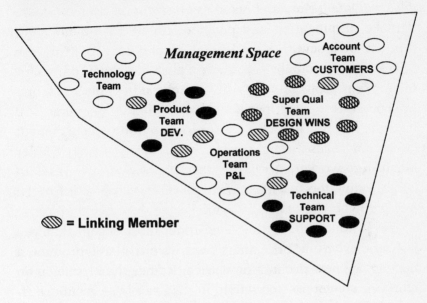

don't own. Conversely, if the cheese is chock full of holes, the chances of it holding together are remote.[7]

Constantly refresh the context. An exciting project consumes people. Once engaged, Silicon Valley knowledge workers have a tendency to put their heads down, focus, and not come up for air until they absolutely have to. With little effort, though, people can lose the context within which their initiative resides. When they finally do pop up for air, they'll look for two data points: First, they'll want to confirm that their project is still valued; and second, they want to see what's coming next.

If they don't see confirmation and a clear next initiative or opportunity, most workers become very unsettled. Some won't go back to their current initiative until they get a satisfactory answer. Others will return to their project, but they will spend most of their time nervously kibitzing with their peers about how management doesn't know what it's doing. Some will appear to be working as they did before, but quietly circulate feelers and resumés among their peer networks to make sure their future is covered. You won't find out about this last group until it's too late.

The trick is to make sure there's always a clear context for the current project and a visible, exciting next project looming ahead. If the next project is truly enticing, of course, it'll take a balancing act to keep workers' attention on the current effort, but this is the right challenge to have. As Tracy Kidder illustrates so eloquently in the classic book *Soul of a New Machine*, innovators are like pinball players: their goal is to get a free game, so they can play again.[8]

Barrier removal. Micromanagement, stupid interruptions, and barriers are what Scott Adams frequently captures in the popular Dilbert comic strip. Adams' strip revolves around how knowledge workers react to being led crudely by seemingly Neanderthal, machine-age managers. A former employee of Pacific Telesis, Adams couldn't find enough creative outlets; as he says, "The corporation is designed to eliminate creativity."[9]

Valley workers want to focus on their work, their hole in the cheese—and anything leaders can do to shield them and their colleagues from extraneous issues, interruptions, and bureaucracy is greatly appreciated. *Nothing you do will score more points than this.* Your help could be as simple as getting them excused from a corporate function that falls during a critical work period, or as complex as trying to minimize the impact of developing next year's annual operating plan. There's no pretty solution to the latter, but whatever can be done to leverage their time will be rewarded.

At the same time, be watchful of knowledge workers' tendency to define their work too narrowly. Left to their own devices, technical knowledge workers will parse the elements of an initiative project into sharply defined pieces. The unstated assumption is that if they divide the task well and everyone does his or her respective piece correctly, the pieces will come together with few problems. In the terms of Swiss cheese management, many face inward within their assigned hole. Such purity rarely works. Leaders, looking at the "white space" between each group's work, will see integration issues before the teams do. To resolve these issues, though, you've got to recognize that the teams don't see the same picture. Get agreement on the issue's existence, and the consequences of not addressing it, before pulling people together to work on it. This will make problem solving much easier.

THE POWER OF PASSION

Since the earliest days of the semiconductor industry, Silicon Valley has forged new ground in defining what knowledge work professionals do, how they do it best, and what drives them to do it. Although it is rarely stated directly as a goal, my experience is that Silicon Valley leaders continually try to evoke, rather than mute, people's passions. Once evoked, the passion is tough to control. It can result in a series of twenty-hour workdays—or, as Scott McNealy and other CEOs have learned, pranks such as your car being placed in the center of the fountain outside your office as a birthday present! The passion to go well beyond the extra mile is what drives people to create insanely great products and services.

Clearly, though, the value of passion has been recognized. Industrial conclaves such as Austin's Silicon Gulch, Oregon's Silicon Forest, and Raleigh Durham's Research Park have mimicked and built on what started here. In addition to these technology centers, companies large and small have started shifting their people management practices to accommodate or support knowledge work and help their people express passion of their own.

ORGANIZING FOR INNOVATION

Innovation in Silicon Valley is not limited to new products and services. In a very fundamental way, the organization structure itself is an integral part of the innovation process. For example, Valley firms are constantly reorganizing—in part because of growth, but more frequently to ensure that the organization conforms to the innovation and other task requirements, rather than the other way around. Nevertheless, the formal framework of most Valley organizations is quite similar to most others'. I'll start this discussion of organization by looking at overall company structure, then rapidly work my way down to the workgroup structure that drives innovation.

Corporate Structure

Long ago, Hewlett-Packard set the pattern for organization in the Silicon Valley. H-P's dominant core organizational entities are divisions, which are aggregated into units such as Test and Measurement Organization. H-P learned early on that when organizations get large, they become unwieldy, distance people from each other, and quickly consume more energy than they release and focus. When Cisco Systems CEO John Chambers looked around for large-scale organizational models that sustained innovation, customer intimacy, and satisfaction, he found Hewlett-Packard's to be the best.

H-P defines a division as a unit having a clear set of customers and competitors. If you can't identify these, then you don't have a division. With few exceptions, most companies follow this basic pattern.

Divisional Structures

In the Valley, what's in a division varies from company to company within the context of two primary models. The first is what you might think of as the complete or stand-alone division. In this case, the division includes or has effective control over every function required to compete; staff functions such as finance and human resources will have a dual reporting structure (to corporate as well as to the division). The second approach is to focus the division on a subset of tasks—usually development and marketing—while keeping others (such as sales and operations/manufacturing) centralized. In either case, divisions have profit and loss responsibility.

One of the dangers divisions present to innovation is that they can create internal competition that thwarts cooperation and learning within the larger firm. When Cisco Systems divisionalized, John Chambers made a point of continuing to reward key executives on the company's overall performance in order to counteract this tendency. Furthermore, Cisco established councils (composed primarily of marketing and sales people) that operate across business units to force cooperation on key innovations, customers, and markets. Other firms, such as Cirrus Logic, use cross-divisional councils as a platform for defining new technologies and defining business strategy.

The Silicon Valley also experiments with companies within, or next to the parent company. For example, Quantum launched Plus Development in the mid-1980s in part to retain key staffers who might have left the corporation and formed a startup of their own. This approach enables companies to create an upside opportunity for people after the growth of the parent has slowed from upwards of 50 percent per year. Using vehicles such as phantom stock, these new entities can provide the feel and reward of a startup. If the business opportunity is significantly different from the parent company, this structure also helps break cultural ties that could get in the way.

A discussion of Valley organization structure would be incomplete without acknowledging the role that formal and informal partnerships play. Since most of the innovations that come out of any one company in the Valley require technology from many others, Valley companies have highly permeable boundaries. Co-locating design and integration talent from parts distributors, storage providers, and chip vendors inside a computer company's facilities is quite common. Joint technology development, as well as marketing agreements, also punch holes in the corporate walls. As these working relationships mature, the operating practices of the Silicon Valley resemble the Japanese *kiretsu* system, without the interlocking ownership.

Internal Company Structure

On paper, the internal structure of a Silicon Valley company or division is probably not different from that of your own company, wherever it is. There are defined functions, such as marketing, sales, and development. Each of these functions is headed by a leader, who sits with other leaders and the general manager to form the division executive staff. That is often the end of any similarity, however.

First, to keep innovation flowing and organization from becoming a barrier, Valley firms are both flat (four levels or less) and fluid. Walls between functions are lower and fewer than they are elsewhere. Adaptability, permeability, and flexibility are as much a state of consciousness as they are a description of how the structure is supposed to work. A Valley organization operates much more like a hockey or European football team than the frequently used metaphor of a symphony orchestra.

People and positions are in constant motion, sometimes moving backward in order to go forward. Each person has certain responsibilities, yet they'll swarm around a problem just like a hockey team attacks a loose puck. As in hockey, you and your project might get knocked down, on purpose or by accident—particularly if you don't keep your head up and watch what's going on around you. Leaders are action-oriented people who charge after problems without waiting for their bosses to identify or approve solutions. The key to being an effective mid-level leader in the Silicon Valley is knowing how to master the informal organization; knowing where to be, and who can contribute regardless of title, is crucial.

Mid-level leaders are like good centers in ice hockey. They set other people up to score, rather than always scoring themselves. In contrast to the rapidly fading model of traditional middle management, controllers or power brokers are not tolerated. In fact, if a Valley middle manager tries to wield power by limiting access or information, people will very quickly subvert his or her authority as they spread the word among their peers.

In the Valley's best companies, people work aggressively and relentlessly within the system as long as it doesn't get in the way. If it does, they'll take responsibility for finding a work around, *and* formerly raising the problem within the existing structure. While they certainly have defined roles and specialties, people function with wide peripheral vision. They specialize in seeing opportunities, and knowing how to keep the formal structure informed while corraling the talent necessary to execute until a problem is fixed.

TEAMS: THE HEART OF INNOVATION

Just as corporate organization structure in the Valley conforms to the task, so does the internal structure. By far, the vast majority of innovation in the Valley occurs in cross-functional teams. Why? Because they are easily structured and customized to bring the right people together for fast, focused development and action. Teams make it easier for partners and suppliers to participate in the innovation effort. Most importantly, since innovation is a pervasively cross-functional process, teams provide a structure that follows the path of least resistance.

Valley management doesn't treat innovation teams as an adjunct to the traditional organization. Instead, management views the team as *the central innovation organization*— and, in the best of cases, defines the role of the functions explicitly as providing support to the teams. Pound for pound, teams in the Silicon Valley have more responsibility, authority, accountability *and capability* than you'll see elsewhere. There's no better example of this than Quantum Corporation.

Quantum established teams in the late 1980s to accomplish two purposes: drive decisions downward, and increase innovation speed via real-time involvement of all relevant functions. They first turned to teams when revenues were less than $500 million and continue to use them today with revenues greater than $4 billion! Michael Brown, Quantum's CEO and one of its first team leaders, credits the teams and establishing divisions as the two changes that have enabled the firm to grow rapidly.

Hold it! Are you starting to skim this chapter because your organization has used multifunctional teams for some time? Are you saying to yourself, "Been there, done that"? Before racing forward, ask yourself these questions to see if the teams in your firm can match Quantum's:

1. Are your teams not only accountable but also resourced with the best the functions have to offer, and looked to by the entire organization—executive staff included—as the central execution vehicle for innovation?
2. Is there a significant difference in the compensation team members receive for their efforts, with an upside (40 percent over base) depending on results?
3. Can your teams give awards up to $15,000 to individuals who *are not on the team* but helped achieve success?
4. Is team participation and leadership the obvious career path for executive positions? At Quantum, the majority of senior management once served on innovation teams.
5. Do executives and functions automatically channel any issue for which the team is responsible, including outside customer inquiries, directly to the team?
6. Are your teams crisply launched? Is there *zero* lag time from when your firm decides to pursue an innovation initiative to when the team is completely staffed and charging forward?
7. Is the natural and ongoing pull between the team's needs and those of the function a source of tension, or has it deteriorated into a source of strained contention?

Very few organizations meet the above criteria. Why are they important? Because when companies view innovation teams as an adjunct structure, they don't change their core practices; functional silos and serial innovation continue to dominate. The reality is that even if you have teams, until you integrate them tightly into how work gets done throughout the company—changing daily behavior and operating practices—you simply don't gain the benefits that accrue to companies like Quantum. And don't be mistaken about the benefits. Effective teams are not the goal; effective innovation for the firm is. Established properly, teams work closely with functions and actually improve functional performance and capabilities.

Here's how this works in the eyes of Quantum's human resources director, Jane Creech. The teams depend on the functions to supply them with capabilities, without which they can't do their job. In fact, if you have a team that's faltering, the first thing you should check is whether the functional capability is present. The team falters when the function's representatives on the team can't deliver function's capabilities, either directly or indirectly. Strong functions make strong teams.

The corollary, though, is also true: strong teams make strong functions. Since the team is the primary forum for innovation delivery, it is accountable to senior management, and every team member's compensation is tied tightly to its results, team members won't tolerate poor functional support. If there's a problem, they'll quickly put pressure on the functions to increase their capabilities. Since senior management defines the function's role as serving the teams, this pressure gets serious attention.

More than those of any organization I know of, Quantum's teams bring alive Michael Porter's metaphor of the value chain. From initial research through end of life, Quantum's interlocking teams form a chain that was illustrated earlier (Figure 6–1). Technology hands off new capabilities (recording head technology, for example), to the product team, which uses it to develop the product. The product team works with the qualification, account, and operations teams to secure initial customers such as Compaq, after which they turn the product over to the operations team to manage until end of life. During its lifetime, the operations team relies on a technical team to provide product support. Each team is composed of those functions whose participation is essential to meet business and customer requirements.

Quantum's teams are relatively small; for example, the product team has seven people on it. This doesn't mean, though, that each product is created by just seven people. Instead, these seven serve as the hub for the hundred or so people who are required to create a new disk drive, forming a decision-making structure that moves fast while also being well informed. The key to Quantum's team structure is that the multifunctional teams provide work direction to many functional resources, rather than the other way around.

Why Teams Underperform or Fail

Why is it, then, that most organizations' attempts at innovation teams fail to deliver the spectacular results that Quantum's achieved? Three key reasons are listed below.

1. *Teams require everyone's attention.* In contrast to almost every other suggestion, tactic, and strategy mentioned in this book as well as others, successfully implementing teams usually requires the active, orchestrated involvement of hundreds of people on an ongoing basis. In contrast, improving the development process or defining and aligning strategy, while not easy, neither involves nor requires such constant, broad participation. But that's also what creates the power in teams—a hundred people working together.
2. *Effective innovation teams require broad changes to organizational reporting relationships, power equations, rewards, and information systems.* In short, you've got to change the organizational equivalent of the firm's "operating system" (be it Unix, DOS, or Microsoft Windows) to be successful.

Most firms undertake teams as though they were merely
another application, such as word processing.

3. *Effective innovation teams require a different mix of capabilities than normally exists.* You'll find that you have too
   few people who possess a general management outlook
   and are also functionally capable. If you're to delegate
   responsibly the amount of authority and accountability
   necessary for success, you *must* have confidence in the
   team members' ability to succeed. No firm, including
   Quantum, ever has enough of these people.

Stopping Team Trouble Before it Starts

Have you had bad experiences with teams? After witnessing
countless implementation efforts, I have found four major
mistakes that can be avoided easily.

Teamitis. This is my name for the uncontrolled proliferation
of teams. The mantra of a firm with acute teamitis is as follows: Have a cold? Get a team! Teamitis strikes most when
management makes it clear that they support teams, yet they
fail to control the number of teams launched. Since management has declared teams to be important, everyone wants to
be on one. Soon every group in the company refers to itself as
a team, and tasks that should be done by individuals become
team tasks.

Teamitis wastes enormous amounts of time and energy.
Quantum nipped this disease in the bud by limiting its official
definition of teams and keeping the number of official teams
small. At Quantum there's no confusion over what a product
team is, or who is on it.

The road warrior syndrome. This occurs when management
uses terms like "empowerment" broadly and doesn't clearly
define team and function boundaries. Named after the ma-
rauding vigilantes in the Australian *Road Warrior* movie series, road warriors operate as though they are in the desert,

commanding four-wheel-drive vehicles equipped with battering rams and rocket launchers. They're willing to blast anything that might get in the way of achieving their goal, even if that means annihilating another team, function, or company goal. You can prevent the rise of road warriors by clearly defining roles and authority among the teams, functions, and senior management.

Ignoring the plumbing. The third error occurs when you implement teams but leave the company infrastructure (such as compensation and information systems) untouched. The most overlooked infrastructure element is the compensation and performance management system. Typically owned and driven by functional leaders, until this system incorporates teams as an integral element, explicit and implied goals conflict. Similarly, if the information system is not rewired so that the teams receive updated information directly, the speed and productivity benefits are lost. You can begin implementation without every element of the plumbing fixed, but these issues must be attended to within the first six months.

Launch, then abdicate. The last mistake occurs when management defines its role simply as launching the teams. As Quantum CEO Michael Brown explains, teams are effective but not very efficient. They require nurturing, monitoring, and ongoing adjustments to keep them working and in line with business strategy. For example, Quantum switched from exclusively having business teams that owned innovation and ongoing operations for a complete product line to a combination of small innovation teams and one operations team for each division. Before the change, the complexity of their operating business had grown such that innovation was no longer getting the attention it required. Today Quantum devotes three people full-time to maintaining the team system; their responsibilities include ensuring that teams can be launched immediately upon project approval, conducting team peer reviews, defining capability gaps, and recommending required changes for the entire structure to senior management. Quantum's senior management assesses the entire structure annually.

VALUES: THE INVISIBLE VALLEY GLUE

Hewlett-Packard is a phenomenal company. How many companies over $30 billion in revenue regularly achieve double-digit growth? H-P doesn't do everything right, but its leaders have an advantage that enables them to adjust and learn as few others can. The depth, breadth, and vitality that come alive daily through the firm's values—the H-P Way—are an asset from which most of the Silicon Valley continues to learn.

As I've noted, you don't lead knowledge workers by telling them what to do. You treat them with respect and dignity, and you provide opportunities that they would not be able to have on their own. Hewlett-Packard's stated values are not uniquely different from most major companies. What makes the H-P Way unique, though, is the seriousness with which values are treated as a management tool. They are not spread by sloganeering, but serve as criteria for daily decision-making and advancement. H-P general managers regularly discuss and assess the vitality of the H-P Way, a process that inevitably results in corrective actions to ensure its continued viability.

Nothing certifies success better than imitation. At Silicon Graphics, Ed McCracken and most of the first generation of executives came from Hewlett-Packard. SGI has its own set of values, for which it annually gives "The Spirit of SGI" awards. Winning employees are nominated and selected by their peers as capturing and promulgating the essence and spirit of SGI values. The prizes include trips to resort locations such as Hawaii.

Why the focus on values? Because they can provide a context that facilitates and enables local, independent action. In today's fast pace, effective self-management and opportunism create a competitive advantage. More importantly, this same pace fragments organizations, gradually destroying what little cohesion and coherence there may have been. A living, vibrant set of values provides the basis for forming and regenerating community. Regardless of the excitement, power, and amazement that today's technologies often evoke, at the end of the day we're all people, with feelings about our efforts, successes, and failures. Brought to life as well as Hewlett-Packard does the H-P Way, values-based management lifts everyone above trivial concerns to focus on those that are truly important.

SUMMARY

If you were to scan the corporate value statements of the Fortune 500, I doubt that you would find many companies that did not state in some way that people were their most important asset. Despite this, the scourge of downsizing that has swept the world suggests that for most firms, these statements are just words.

Silicon Valley has its poor performers, living dead, and badly managed firms like anywhere else, but there are some differences. One palpable difference is that people really do come first in the Valley. In part, it's because the Valley is really quite small and incestuous, and with a little effort you can always find someone who knows someone who works at a given company. With the exception of the occasional recession, people are mobile, and this places a burden on management to provide an environment where work is rewarding and fun. In turn, this legacy of managing knowledge workers—each of whom possesses several employment alternatives—keeps the focus on people. This legacy illustrates why innovation in the Silicon Valley extends far beyond the technology itself.

7

Measuring Your
Measurement System

Simplicity applies to measurements also. Too often we measure
everything and understand nothing.
—Jack Welch, CEO, General Electric Company

Imagine that you're an adviser to one of Quantum's development teams, working on a next-generation disk drive. At today's meeting, they're defining what variables they should measure to guarantee that their initiative meets its objectives. During the discussion, they turn to you with a question: Should we track the cost of the development effort?

Before you volunteer an answer, let me give you a few facts. A typical new platform product takes approximately a year to develop and involves approximately 100 people. A rough estimate of the average development cost of a new drive is $25 million; sales can easily cross the billion-dollar mark within four quarters. Like all Quantum developments, the engineering will be done in the Valley, and the manufacturing will be done by Matsushita's MKE division in Asia. Along the way, the team will build several prototype lots, each of which is quite expensive.

So, should the team track the development program's cost? Most executives in my Stanford and Caltech classes say yes, frequently citing the five classic metrics for innovation programs: performance, schedule, quality, product/service cost, and (of course) development cost. Not to address this cost seems irresponsible, particularly when you consider the rough estimate of $25 million.

The team came to the same conclusion, but they stopped measuring approximately four months into the program. They ran into a common problem in today's organizations: the data were difficult to get, incomplete, and not very accurate. Most corporations' measurement systems do a far better job of providing summary data to outsiders, such as the auditors and the SEC, than they do of providing it to those who run the business.

By and large, performance measurement and accounting systems have remained relatively unchanged in this century. Despite the dramatic changes in business philosophy, strategy, and operations brought about by intense competition, re-engineering, and the pressures of the global knowledge economy, we are using the same measures—and, more importantly, the same measurement mindset—that Henry Ford used to run the historic Rouge plant that built the Model T.

In this chapter I will address the final element of the innovation system, measurement. While innovation measurement has advanced in the Silicon Valley on a relative basis, everyone could stand to improve significantly. I'll begin by defining the role measurement plays in innovation, identifying the classic innovation measurements, and highlighting useful new measures from the Silicon Valley. Next I'll discuss the value of predictive measures and show you how to create them. Then I'll turn to how we use measures and identify the most common mistakes, paying particular attention to what I refer to as the measurement mindset. Here you will see that what the Quantum team eventually decided to do makes perfect sense, and you'll better understand the measurement mess in which most firms find themselves. I'll close the chapter by presenting an alternative model for using measures, using the experience of Cirrus Logic to do so.

THE ROLE OF INNOVATION MEASUREMENT: GUIDE, FOREWARN, AND INFORM

The basic purpose of any measurement system is to provide feedback, relative to some goals, that increases your chances of achieving these goals efficiently and effectively. Measurement is only a tool, it gains true value when used as the basis for timely decisions. That said, measurement fulfills three primary roles, as outlined below.

Guide. Measurement provides data for course corrections to create a winning product or service *across the entire value proposition.* Many firms approach course correction too narrowly by focusing only on the original value proposition, as reflected by such internal surrogates as schedule, features, timing, cost, and quality targets. If the world stood still throughout the development and your original targets were pinpoint-accurate from the start, this approach would work. That's a mighty big if, of course.

In practice, you are almost guaranteed that technology advances, competitors' actions, and customers' understanding of what they want will change from the time you start the project until you're finished. If you collect data and adjust based only on your original target, you might be deadly accurate but equally unsuccessful. To be successful in the market, you must also test whether the original targets still define what it takes to win. Since you can count on change occurring, your constant challenge will be deciding what to do, if anything, based on the new information you receive.

Forewarn. In the best case, your measurement system can forewarn you of problems *before* you hit them and illuminate potential alternatives. This is where the measurement system is worth its weight in gold. At the same time, traditional innovation measures emphasize results and are not predictive; to predict, you have to understand the process and technology variables that cause problems. These are not always intuitively obvious, yet through process mapping and disciplined postmortems, they are much easier to identify than you might think. (I'll explore predictive measures in greater depth later in this chapter.)

Inform. When the results are widely available, innovation measurement keeps others informed of the initiative's progress so they can coordinate their efforts. This is particularly important as firms increasingly undertake tasks in parallel, both within and between initiatives. For example, if you're going to be a couple of months early (don't laugh, it can happen!), then sales might not be ready to support the launch. Informing a wider audience, though, is a dual-edged sword. It provides an opening for others to provide counsel and help, some of which is not always considered helpful by those receiving it.

What Basic Measures Should I Use?

The five classic results measures to watch are as follows:

1. Performance
2. Quality
3. Timing
4. Financials: cost, margins and revenue
5. Development cost

Performance. How well does the total solution perform, relative to customer requirements and competitive offerings? In each industry, the variables that define performance will vary; in the financial services industry, return, risk, liquidity, and convenience are four common performance measures. Performance measures are most effective when they are grounded in customer and market data rather than tied to internal benchmarks (such as a degree of improvement over what is currently available). Displays such as spider diagrams (see Figure 7–1) are far more compelling portrayals than spreadsheets, because they graphically illustrate the relationships between variables.

Quality. Quality is a tricky beast, because the devoted define it as anything that leads to or could impair customer satisfaction. While this is true, the definition is too all-encompassing for use as the basis of measurement. A less robust but more useful approach targets defects that hinder the usability and reliability of the solution. For example, inaccurate monthly statements would be a defect for a new financial investment.

Timing. Once the initiative begins, the daily reference point for timing rapidly shifts from what the market requires to

FIGURE 7–1

Spider Diagram

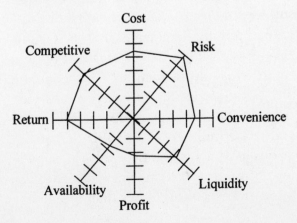

what is defined in the schedule. So much effort is required to develop and manage the internal schedule that it is very easy to lose sight of the more critical issue: customer and market timing. Accurately predicting and maintaining a schedule makes internal coordination easier, but it has little value if you miss in the marketplace.

In the Silicon Valley, people frequently assume that faster is better. This is often true, but there are times when the best way to go fast is to start slowly. With software tools such as Microsoft Project, one can conduct a what-if (or "critical path") analysis that can help determine the overall impact of speeding up or slowing down specific tasks. Increasingly easy to use, this software brings a higher level of insight and disciplined thinking to innovation timing.

Financials. This category includes product or service cost, margins, and revenue expectations. Cost often receives more detailed attention in manufacturing than in service innovation, but that's changing. As global competition squeezes profit margins everywhere, the cost parameters of service are becoming increasingly important; health care is a perfect example. In the manufacturing sector, 90 percent of a product's cost is determined in development, with as much as half of that coming from suppliers. Despite the fact that they have little leverage, manufacturing groups are normally held accountable for cost once the product is in production.

Just as the target of any innovation effort should be a complete solution, it's increasingly important that this same thinking be applied to cost. Traditional cost accounting was designed for a manufacturing environment where production facilities ran full tilt, and the majority of costs were direct. Knowledge work turns the equation upside down, since more than 80 percent of costs are indirect. As you will see shortly, this is one of the reasons most firms find themselves in a measurement mess—our accounting systems were designed for conditions that are now the exception rather than the rule.

Development cost. Development cost brings us back to the Quantum team discussion. Certainly, if your innovation costs run into the hundreds of millions (as they do in aerospace or autos), you should pay attention to the development cost. In Quantum's case, though, the development cost is significant but very difficult to trace. Like most firms, Quantum uses a traditional periodic accounting system that captures costs using departmental codes. Only where codes are used for specific projects, such as prototype builds and dedicated engineering resources, are these costs traceable. Most of the development costs are indirect and not traceable.

And that's just half the story. In addition, the degree of control Quantum's development teams have over development cost is quite limited. For example, if an initiative got into such technical trouble that additional prototype lots were required to solve the problem, there would be little question if the lots should be run. The consequences of missing the market window for Quantum are far greater than a cost overrun. From an overall perspective, Quantum's aggregate development costs are a function of the number of projects they commit to during any period.

Popular Measures Used in the Valley

Cycle time. Throughout the Silicon Valley, fast cycle time has become a competitive must.[1] Cycle time defines how long it takes to complete a repeatable process. In addition to the total innovation cycle, companies measure critical subcycles throughout their business. Cycle time measures are used for process improvement as well as as a predictor of overall development speed and schedule capability. Besides being congruent with the Valley's relentless innovation pace, cycle time measures drive quality improvement, since you can't be fast if you generate a lot of rework.

Cycle time is also a very easy metric to establish and explain. Everyone from top to bottom understands both the value of time and how to track it; all you need to do is define the beginning and end of the process and buy a watch. To measure cycle time in tangible work areas like manufacturing is very easy. In knowledge work, the middle of the cycle is usually clear, but defining the start and finish is a less precise art. Even so, more and more companies are using cycle time in innovation.

An interesting twist that Unisys has used is measuring the time to first failure—or, in software, the time required to find the first thousand bugs. The logic is that during the early innovation phases, there will be problems and bugs. By reducing the time to uncover as many problems as possible, you flush tough issues out into the open more quickly and speed up learning. Hewlett-Packard uses a similar approach for products, which they call "strife" testing. Here the objective is to push the product to the breaking point in order to discover its weak points.

Resource capability. Long ago, Intel recognized that rapid growth often causes jobs to grow in scope and requirements more quickly than the people in them can keep up. In addition to measuring current performance, Intel assesses people's "bandwidth" or capabilities relative to the expanded scope of their current job, as well as assessing future capacity. For example, your performance in your current job could be well above average today, but at the rate the job is expanding, you might be stretched beyond your capabilities in a year. Thus you would receive rewards for above average performance based on your current achievements, but your manager would also watch how you handle the job as it expands. If there are bandwidth concerns, you probably won't be promoted, even though your current performance is well above average.

Cisco Systems takes a different, but also intriguing, approach to address capability growth. As competitive pressures increase throughout the Valley, it's harder for firms to fill job openings. Companies like Cisco have more than five hundred openings during peak growth periods. Although recruitment is important, it frequently takes second place to daily business. Recognizing that this tendency could cripple Cisco's growth, CEO John Chambers set goals supported by a measure that compares the current head count to the authorized head count, for which a target percentage is set. The goal, supported by the measure, keeps a focus on hiring all the way to the top.

Surprisingly, with all the effort human resource professionals have put into performance appraisal, there are few systemic approaches for defining the capabilities a firm needs to win and comparing them to what it has on hand. Several companies, led by Skandia of Sweden, have started to measure their firm's knowledge base as a business asset. The next step is a real-time gap analysis between competitive intellectual capital requirements and current intellectual capital.

Resource capacity. Efforts to monitor the match between aggregate innovation resource requirements and capacity are becoming increasingly prevalent in the Silicon Valley. Since I've discussed this at length in an earlier chapter, I won't go into detail here. One of the Valley's strongest proponents of this trend, Cirrus Logic's CEO Mike Hackworth, believes that resource overloading was the primary contributor to two quarters of reported losses in early 1996. Those who address resource capacity use rules of thumb for such basic initiative types as breakthroughs, platforms, and line extensions. The rules of thumb define the average resource requirement for each.

Team effectiveness. Due to the pivotal role multifunctional teams play in Valley innovation, companies like Quantum and Sun Microsystems pay close attention to team effectiveness. This occurs within the team as well as through outside experts. A common mistake is to converge on how well the team gets along. This is certainly relevant, but far more important is how well the team works together to achieve its goals. Few companies approach the task from a business perspective as well as Quantum does with its combination of peer review, executive sponsor, and external assessment.

Competitive comparisons. Dell Computer's innovation teams track and continuously compare their new initiatives to current competitor products, new introductions, and announcements. Hewlett-Packard and IBM, among others, regularly compare bills of materials, part counts, standard versus custom part usage, and estimated processing costs by tearing down competitor products as soon as the latter are available. The key in both these cases is that these tear-downs and benchmarking efforts are linked and incorporated into the innovation teams' tracking measures.

The value of these metrics can greatly increase innovation effectiveness. Through such tear-downs during the heyday of the dot matrix printer, IBM learned that the printer made by Epson, its initial supplier, was exceedingly complicated with more than 150 parts. IBM launched a team with a simplification goal and knocked the part count down to 62, cutting assembly from thirty minutes to only three.

INNOVATION RADAR: THE POWER OF PREDICTIVE MEASURES

By the time you find yourself in trouble on any of the five classic results measures cited above, frequently you know very little about how you got there or when the problem started. As a manager, once you discover that a desired result has gone south, how, when, and what are you going to do about it are the topics that dominate the conversation. For example, an 8 percent drop in quarterly profits accompanied by a 10 percent rise in service costs does not tell a customer service team what its service technicians should do differently on their next call. Predictive measures, however, examine the actions and capabilities that contributed to the situation. Knowing that several new technician hires dropped the average skill level such that the average time spent per service call rose 15 percent—and that, as a result, the number of late calls rose 10 percent—would explain why service costs had gone up and customer satisfaction and profits had gone down.

The question of when problems are discovered is critical, particularly in a turbulent environment. Every day an error stays undetected, more effort and resources are required to right the situation. Predictive measures help you detect trouble faster—or, better yet, halt its progress early. In the following paragraphs I'll provide some proven examples of predictive measures, then show you how you can create others on your own. The predictive measures shown in Figure 7–2 work! I've seen all of them used effectively in manufacturing. Several, such as turnover, directly apply to service.

Creating Your Own Process Measures

There are four basic steps to creating process measures: defining what results are important, mapping the cross-functional process used to deliver results, identifying the critical tasks and capabilities required to complete the process successfully, and designing measures that track those tasks and capabilities.[2] The most effective process measures are often those that express relative terms. A measure that tracks the percentage of inexperienced people, for example, is usually more valuable than one that tracks the absolute number.

For example, in Cirrus Logic's Graphics Company chip business, getting the correct feature set to the market on time is critical. In a comprehensive innovation improvement and cycle time reduction effort, the Graphics Company mapped its innovation process as it was executed on the last three major products. When the maps were analyzed, it became clear that although customers' requirements often shifted over the course of development, too frequently Cirrus's designers had not taken a clear position on features within their own teams. Of the many variables involved, two stood out. First, whenever the primary architect of the product was not

FIGURE 7-2

Predictive Measures

Measure	Impact
Cycle time	Slow cycle times of key subprocesses (e.g., field test), can surface problems, or overly aggressive or unrealistic schedules.
Percent of tests passed	Continuing test failures reflect slow product/service maturity and learning within the team.
Turnover	Turnover increases workload per person remaining, plus new hires dilute average productivity until they gain experience on the initiative.
Specification changes	Every change takes time to decide and execute that is added to the original work plan. Changing one element usually causes problems with others.
Requirement changes	Each request takes time and energy away from the original work plan. If changed, specification changes and their consequence follow.
Percent of modules reused	Reused modules or components are familiar and proven. The higher the level of reuse, the faster and more likely the design will work
Percent of new parts	Adds supplier, integration, and technology risk that can quickly extend development. Production may suffer from shortages or handling inexperience.
Percent of unique parts	Potential supplier, integration, and technical delays with limited expertise to solve.
Percent of new vendors	Many new suppliers compound procurement, testing, integration, and manufacturing.
Percent of staffed to plan	Slow staffing means delays due to incomplete work or rework when permanent staff arrives and changes what's been done to date.
Percent of time lost to other projects/support	If you're spending time on something else, guess what suffers?

fully engaged or available during definition, programs had more problems. Second, the definition process was fragmented between many people and inadequately addressed known interdependencies among market, technology, manufacturing, and service requirements.

As part of its improvement efforts, the Graphics Company adopted a more rigorous definition process staffers refer to as their "contract book." The contract book is much more robust than a schedule, and it serves as a comprehensive, evergreen definition of the complete program. When Cirrus created team measurements, it included two predictive measures. The first assesses the ongoing completeness of the contract book, and the second focuses on the three most critical resource gaps. The contract book measure of completeness uses a gauge beginning with "danger" and ending with "good shape." The resource gauges display present staffing compared to resource requirements, both near and long term. In the early phase, architects are a resource that is tracked.

Measurement Mistakes

Measurement errors fall into two broad categories that aren't totally discrete. The first category emphasizes the consequence of misuse at a local or individual level; the second category looks at what happens when misuse becomes a pattern. I'll quickly highlight the most common local measurement errors and then focus my attention on the patterns of misuse, for this is a far more serious and intractable problem.

Each of the local errors cited below will be familiar to you. Each error has its own nuance, yet taken together they all reflect incomplete understanding or wavering application discipline.

1. *The classic mistakes.* Inaccurate, late or unreliable data.
2. *On again, off again.* Not measuring at all, or doing so inconsistently or incompletely. This is the "seat-of-the-pants" approach, more frequently found in nontechnical areas that assert variables are hard to measure, so why bother?

3. *Video game measurement.* The focus is on hitting the number like a target in a video game, ignoring the purpose behind the number. This error also applies to using measures to draw conclusions without understanding what the measures reflect.

4. *One measure fits all.* This usually occurs when lower-level operations use the same measurement that senior management uses for summary information, even though the former are only responsible for a piece. For example, because an innovation team usually doesn't have control over all costs, it should focus on those elements it does control (like bill of materials, or the specific steps in the service process).

5. *Mistake the measure for reality.* Most measures are surrogates for a result or a behavior, and individually are not complete or accurate. For example, development schedule requirements as defined in a product/service definition become the company's internal clock, whereas customers follow an external market clock that often is different.

6. *Shooting the messenger.* This is the quickest way to stop measurement from spreading throughout your company. As Cirrus Logic's Mike Hackworth says, "Now and then, you've got to eat 'reality cookies.' If we know the real story, we can prepare Wall Street analysts rather than surprising them."

While these problems surface locally, the root cause is not local. This is why we're in a measurement mess, as I'll explain in the next section.

THE MEASUREMENT MESS: WHY PEOPLE RESIST MEASUREMENT

Ever since I encountered resistance to creating cycle time measures over eight years ago, people's love-hate of measurement practices has been a fascination as well as an area of research and study for me. Fasten your seat belt and crank up your cranial horsepower, because in the next section I'm going to wade you through a swamp that has been mostly ignored by all the organization transformation and reengineering work. Since wading through swamps does not strike most people as an appealing way to spend their time, let me tell you why you should come along.

If we think of organizations as being organic, then the measurement system is the equivalent of the central nervous system. If the data in the nervous system are bad, or the processing breaks between the synapses, nerves, and brain, you're in trouble. You're also in trouble if the messages sent back to the muscles are faulty. In either event, we'll make bad decisions while thinking that they're good. My argument is that we're doing this frequently, if not regularly. See for yourself.

How Big Is the Measurement Mess?

To size the extent of the measurement mess within your company, ask yourself the following questions:

1. What role does innovation play in your competitive strategy?
2. What is necessary for effective innovation?
3. What does your firm measure?
4. Does your current measurement system drive change, or simply maintain the status quo?

The most popular answer to the first question is that innovation is essential for competitiveness and growth. People answer what's necessary for effective innovation with a broad list that usually includes capabilities, learning, money, technology, time to market, and strategic alliances. The third question unearths the first signs of trouble. With the exception of money, few companies have any measures that track the other responses to question two. A few companies have begun to address this, but even in those, the dominance of traditional financial measures continues. In response to the fourth question, rarely does anyone say that their firm's measurement system drives change. Most quickly agree that today's performance measurement systems primarily reinforce and sustain the status quo; that, by itself, has serious implications for innovation. The last two answers, taken together, paint a more disturbing picture.

What's Wrong: Nothing's Changed for Fifty Years

With a few notable exceptions, today's measurement practices and strategies are fundamentally unchanged from fifty years ago. Originally designed to support the command-and-control paradigm, they collected data locally and forward it to top management's command center for review and decision. The resulting decision is communicated out to the troops for execution. As in the mainframe computing model, analysis and decision making is centralized.

Contrast this with the decentralized and distributed power structures that earmark fast, innovative organizations. Rather than being subjected to remote analysis, data should be collected, analyzed, and acted upon locally. It's faster, it uses the resources that have the most relevant knowledge, and most importantly, it retains ownership for whatever actions are taken. In the old model, once you forward data upward, you have little ownership for what's decided—thus, when it comes to execution, is it any wonder that commitment is hard to generate?

Left unchanged, the traditional measurement model reminds me of a silent dog whistle. While management publicly proclaims the importance of speed, innovation, and empowerment, the outdated measurement system silently transmits a loud and contradictory command-and-control ringing in *all* employees' ears. The problems this causes are many. In short, we measure most that which matters least, as detailed below:

• *Precision.* We're inclined to measure what's easy to measure with precision, rather than what is important but imprecise.

Consequently, we grow explicit knowledge and lag in tacit knowledge. For example, while capabilities, environment, and creativity are essential for innovation, rarely are these measured, nor do they become improvement targets until a crisis hits. We collect data about the "hard" problems, but it's the "soft" issues that we struggle with most.

- *Direct labor.* Most measurement systems focus on direct labor, even though well over 80 percent of innovation and knowledge work is indirect. Similarly, we measure capital equipment utilization, when throughput speed and quality are the more vital competitive factors.
- *Change.* Even in those rare situations where we do measure less tangible elements, such as intellectual capital, we measure what we have or lack, rather than the rate of acquisition or depreciation. Since the knowledge required to compete increases daily, and left alone, depreciates rapidly, without knowing the rate of increase or erosion, you only have half the picture.
- *Money.* Money is the common denominator of business, but often it's an overused surrogate. We need balanced measurement systems that also include customer satisfaction, learning, and capabilities.[3]
- *Who spent the money?* Far more important than which departmental code or cost center is charged is, what was the purpose of the expenditure? Did the expenditure add value? Human effort, using resources and leveraged through organization processes, creates customer value. Though available, most companies still do not use activity-based accounting systems, and those that do use them primarily in manufacturing.

To underscore how important these problems are, look at the difference between the data you would use to make a personal career decision versus what we use to manage innovation and run our companies in general. If you were lured by a headhunter to interview at another firm, you would combine hard data on the firm's performance with all the other data you picked up during your visit. This could include a conversation you overheard in the bathroom, whether you were kept waiting for a scheduled interview, the overall appearance of the work environment, your impression of their strategy, and so on. You might also ask your friends and loved ones for their opinion.

In short, you'd be willing to make a life-changing decision using primarily soft data. Yet when you return to your current job, I'm willing to bet that many of the variables that you considered in your decision to stay or leave are not part of your current measurement system. Get the picture? When our career is on the line, our definition and set of useful data are significantly larger than what we use to manage.

Numbers *Do* Lie

Robert Kaplan, the architect of activity-based accounting, created the first financial management tool that recognized the shift in work from brawn to brains. The primary difference between his activity-based model and traditional accounting is that the activity-based model allocates cost based on activities (such as a customer visit) instead of categories (such as rent). What might sound like a small and uninteresting accounting detail has significant impact on your firm's ability to innovate.

Here's a simple example Tony Hope uses to explain the difference.[4] A typical budget for a sales office might have cost categories such as salaries, benefits, rent, telephone, and travel. None of these say anything about what the salesperson does. If economic pressures forced you to reduce spending 10 percent in this sales office, what would you cut? Your only real choices are travel and possibly telephone expenses. Aren't these the salespersons' primary tools? And so we see that traditional accounting works well for the accountant, but it provides little useful data to those who manage.

What if you tracked the activities that generated cost? The same budget could be broken into customer visits, in-company meetings, time spent defining next-generation products/services, and, of course, time spent chasing the factory or operations. Not only is this more accurate, it exposes problems and opportunities. Traditional accounting provides no visibility into chasing the factory, or too little effort on a new initiative development. Isn't one of the biggest problems in innovation getting good input from the field? When Hewlett-Packard installed activity-based accounting in its United Kingdom sales office, it quickly discovered that instead of spending what was estimated at 30 percent of their time with customers, sales representatives were only spending 7 percent. Most of the time that was thought to be in customer contact was consumed in chasing the factory, credit approvals, and other non-value-added tasks.

The problems cited above are vibrantly alive and well in companies throughout the world. Yet I would argue that just changing the measures will not clean up the measurement mess, because it is also inside us. It's in how we think about and use the measures we have. Ever see a messenger shot while delivering bad news?

The Mindset of Control: Shooting the Messenger

When people discuss performance measurement, invariably the conversation turns into a quest for the right or, better yet, perfect measure. The implicit undertone is that if we could just figure out the right measure, especially for those important but softer issues, all measurement problems would be solved. The unstated definition of what the right measure would look like is one that has precision and objectivity, with which no one would disagree. Is there such a measure, or are we really trying to provide the messenger with a bulletproof vest?

The quest for precision and objectivity are red herrings. The fact is, you can measure anything. We acknowledge this whenever we read a movie or restaurant review (three stars are better than two). *The problem people have with measures is not the actual metric or results achieved; it is how the mea-*

sures will be interpreted and used. At the same time, engaging in an open discussion about how measures are or will be used is not a conversation that many people consider safe to have. In the wise words of Chris Argyris, the problem is one that's not discussible.[5] Doing so finds you wading deep into other people's motivations and trust. That's what this swamp is all about. To cope with our discomfort, we steer the discussion into this seemingly well-intentioned search for the right measure. It's an elegantly evasive, yet endless, dance.

Why are people so concerned with how measures will be used? That's easy. Our organization's morgues are still receiving messengers shot while delivering the numbers. Although we talk about the importance of measurement for learning, the mindset is too often measurement for control. If you doubt this, consider one of the most common management aphorisms: "If you want to get something done, create a measure for it." In other words, if you want to make sure people will do what you want, tell them you're going to check on them. Why doesn't it go, "If you want to get something done, set a goal"? Goals establish what you want to accomplish, whereas measures guide and track your progress to goals.

Crafting better measures is not nearly as big a problem as the measurement mindset used to interpret and act on them. If the measures improve but the mindset doesn't, people will continue to shy away from using measures. The measurement mindset in use by most firms represents the strongest remaining element of the traditional command-and-control paradigm: measures are a top-down surrogate for control. Today, organizations rarely use measures for learning.

Implications for Innovation

Are the lingering issues of the command-and-control mindset important? You bet. Since knowledge is increasingly the core component of customer value, how effectively a firm learns impacts its ability to innovate and can often can determine its competitive standing. Secondly, control and innovation are like oil and water. Innovation needs space to experiment and freedom to fail. The consequence of command-and-control measurement is that people stop creating and start complying.

Create or comply? When the measurement mindset is control, employees stop thinking about winning through creating customer value, and focus on winning the internal measurement game. Just look at what happens during an innovation team's status report. If the subject has anything to do with money or schedule, the format will have three columns: budgeted, actual, and, of course, variance. When people read these reports, most read going from right to left, usually starting with the first negative variance. The operating assumption is that negative variances are bad. Late is bad, on schedule is good, and early is better. Sound familiar?

What if being *seriously* overbudget enabled a product or service to avoid missing a critical market window? Research at McKinsey suggests that in fast-moving markets, hitting the window on time—even if spending was 50 percent over-budget—only reduces total profits for that product (they didn't discuss service) by 3 percent. In contrast, being on budget but six months late reduces profits by approximately 30 percent. Under a different set of conditions, you might choose to be late *if* it enabled you to include a blockbuster feature based on technology that wasn't available to your competitors. Measures provide data, not answers. In command-and-control environments, people treat the target as the answer, and they use the measure as the vehicle to hit it.

There's nothing wrong and everything right about setting targets, as long we remain clear that they are *predictions* of what we expect will be the best answer, not absolute statements of fact. For example, budget targets are set at the beginning of the year, yet in turbulent environments who's to say that our wisdom in establishing targets is still valid six or eleven months later? Or, if the firm's growing significantly faster, does it make sense to use the same budget targets? Systems theorists such as Peter Senge demonstrate clearly that underinvestment in capacity and capabilities limits growth. It's the same dynamic as having a development freeway that's too small relative to the number of cars; innovation and growth grind to a halt.

Measuring left of the decimal point: Hurdle rates, learning, stretch and prediction. Today's measurement systems have a strong, and often negative, impact on innovation. Let's start with the drive for measurement precision. Innovation is an imprecise science. If you're required to pinpoint the risks, dimensions, and opportunities with the same precision that you apply to analyzing yesterday's spending, you'll only work on those innovations that you already know a lot about, thereby squeezing out breakthrough and platform efforts. Hewlett-Packard's early cycle time reduction efforts did this, as people found that the way to shorten time to market was to drastically limit innovation stretch. Innovation lives to the left of the decimal point.

The strategic value of hurdle rates, which are based on the current accounting conventions, is increasingly questionable. The inaccuracies of a traditional accounting system can establish hurdle rates either higher or lower than intentions. In addition, high hurdle rates also skew companies from innovations for which the ability to predict the return is low. In fact, since R&D is expensed in the United States, the fast route to increased profits is less R&D investment! In response, companies such as Merck consider R&D internally as capital investment.

WHAT SHOULD I DO DIFFERENTLY?
A PROPOSAL FOR KNOWLEDGE
WORK MEASUREMENT

There is no question that more and more companies are beginning to experience the problems that an outdated measurement system causes. Large Fortune 500 firms such as Merck, Skandia, and Dow Chemical are all in the process of changing their approach to measurement. In the words of Merck & Company's CFO Judy Lewent, "The accounting system doesn't capture anything, really." Thus the first and most obvious step is to move to an activity-based accounting and management system. There are an increasing number of software vendors and consultants, from the big accounting firms on down, that can help you achieve this.

Next, we need to reset our measurement philosophy from command and control to one that supports fast, globally distributed organizations. To that end, the following defines the five tenets for a knowledge work measurement system. To truly adopt it, you'll first have to have the undiscussible discussion of the hidden, controlling side of measurement. If you don't, it's unlikely people will see the importance and value of this new approach.

- *Focus on the critical few.* Get away from piles of numbers and define the minimum set of balanced measures (financial, learning, customer satisfaction, and business capabilities/infrastructure). Worry less about precision and objectivity and more about measuring the critical factors as best you can.
- *Develop measures and align based on strategic objectives.* Senior management's role is to ensure that measures that are developed and used support the firm's objectives. Common measures should be used only where they clearly add value.
- *Emphasize local design and use.* Whenever possible, data and measures should be defined, collected, analyzed, and acted upon in the same place.
- *Use measurement for learning.* Dramatically increase the learning component within the measurement system by adopting a more "clinical" approach to data. Senior management must be willing to eat "reality cookies" to encourage the truthful use of measures.
- *Real-time and accurate.* Eliminate lag time between when the data exit and when they're captured and usable for de-

cisions. Accuracy means that where soft are used, the degree of precision is defined.

To bring life to these tenets, let's return to the Valley and visit Cirrus Logic to see how it has begun to implement this new approach using the team dashboard.

THE INNOVATION TEAM DASHBOARD

As I noted in an earlier work, multifunctional teams need their own measurement system if they are to succeed.[6] The existing system is command-and-control focused, plus the vast majority of measures reflect single-function needs. Left as they are, the separate functional measurements pull the team apart, negating the value of the multifunctional composition. Conflicting goals remain invisible. Even more importantly, without a team measurement system, the team is essentially flying blind. As a result, it's extraordinarily difficult for the team to give senior management a sense of confidence that they are on top of the situation. If they can't do that, it's only a matter of time before management begins to meddle in the team.

The vehicle dashboard (Figure 7–3) is a compelling metaphor for a team-based measurement system. You don't read a dashboard; you glance at it for Using real-time gauges such as fuel, and historical gauges such as the odometer, the dashboard efficiently displays highly relevant and useful data.

FIGURE 7–3

Dashboard

Thus, several years ago, my colleagues and I began building locally defined team dashboards as one step toward the creation of a knowledge work measurement system. Cirrus Logic not only adopted the concept but helped us take it one step further by incorporating it into the company intranet.

The Cirrus Logic Team Dashboard

Cirrus Logic makes chips for the fast-moving PC market, using multifunctional development teams. Cirrus grew very rapidly due to acquisitions. The acquisition strategy was technology-driven, aimed at assembling the critical technologies required to sustain leadership in PC semiconductors. Cirrus is organized into companies, each of whom targets a specific market (such as mass storage, audio, or PC graphics). Winning in any one of these markets requires the free flow of technology across these internal companies.

As you might imagine, growing this way has created a polyglot of cultures, development methodologies, and tools. As part of its effort to reduce cycle time and improve innovation, Cirrus has carefully nudged each company to a limited, common set of innovation practices. One of these, the team dashboard, has been particularly impactful both in how it was developed and how it is used.

Today, each innovation team maintains a dashboard that tracks the critical variables relative to its initiative. The dashboard includes predictive metrics for cycle time, staffing, specification stability, and contract book completeness, plus an open section for major obstacles. It was developed with input from each of the companies and senior management. The dashboard definition process forced individual companies and Cirrus leadership to define some common terminology, as well as to agree about what was important. It's fair to say that the process began from the bottom up, but it was completed with some top-down tiebreaking.

The process of reaching agreement on the measures forced a dialogue between management and the teams, as well as

FIGURE 7–4

Product Dashboard

Dashboard For:

Product Goal: <Brief product description and marketplace goals>

Overall Status

Cycle Time In Months From Concept to Capacity

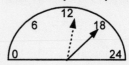

Stability of Features & Product Spec

Process / Design Book

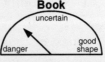

Production Silicon

Key Customers & Markets

	Prob of Sale	Initial Contact	Req's Defined	Samples Required	Volume Prod
Compaq		date	date	date	date
NEC		date	date	date	date
IBM		date	date	date	date

Business Goals

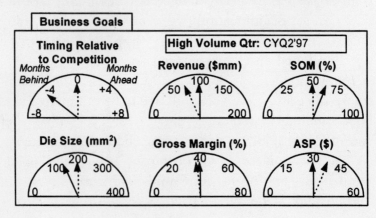

Timing Relative to Competition

High Volume Qtr: CYQ2'97

Revenue ($mm)

SOM (%)

Die Size (mm^2)

Gross Margin (%)

ASP ($)

FIGURE 7–4

(Continued)

Date:

	Target Market: <Segment Targeted>	
	Process: TZM	**Package:** BGA

Critical Barriers & Actions

1)	Owner:
	Due Date:
2)	Owner:
	Due Date:
3)	Owner:
	Due Date:

Staffing

Total FTEs required vs actual FTEs on hand

Short term: Months 1-3 · Long term: Months 4-6

Size (FTEs)		Last Mon	This Mon
of 3 most critical gaps	IC Design	#	#
	Analog	#	#
	Drivers	#	#

	Last Mon	This Mon
Validation	#	#
Drivers	#	#
Bios	#	#

Team Execution

Activity	Overall Status	Next Milestone	Date Due	Prob On-Time	Missed / Total ARs
Definition / Specs		milestone	date	%	# / #
Marketing		milestone	date	%	# / #
Hardware Impl & Verif		milestone	date	%	# / #
Software Development		milestone	date	%	# / #
Validation & S/W Q/A		milestone	date	%	# / #
Manufacturing		milestone	date	%	# / #

Key: Shading = key change from last month ····▶ Dotted = target value ——▶ Solid = current est of value among some of the teams, about what measures were important and why. The dialogue helped bring team members closer together as they learned what was important in the eyes of the other functions. People strongly resisted measuring anything exclusively for senior management's benefit; to be included, each measure had to prove it was useful to the team running the project. As always happens, some compromises were made, but the overall outcome was a significant and positive step forward.

Each team updates its dashboard every two weeks and posts it on the Cirrus intranet; anyone who wants to check on a program's status simply goes to the team's home page and clicks on the dashboard link. The teams use the dashboards, in conjunction with other more specific functional measures, to guide their efforts. Senior management uses them to understand individual program status quickly, as well as to develop an aggregate view around issues such as staffing.

Lessons Learned from Cirrus

We learned many lessons during the creation of the Cirrus Logic dashboards. They reflect the promise that the new measurement model brings, as well as the tenacity with which the command-and-control model survives:

1. *Overmeasurement.* The bias was always to include another measure, rather than test if it added value.
2. *Control.* Senior management had frequent moments of infatuation, seeing the dashboard as a way to peer down into the teams rather than have it be a tool for the team first and management second.
3. *Automation.* Until we automated the dashboard so that the gauges were generated automatically, people continually complained it was too much trouble.
4. *Creative "suction."* The concept expanded beyond one Cirrus company when senior management began to ask for the data on a regular basis. Until then, teams adopted

the on-again, off-again approach to measurement. Once someone important cared, adoption became much easier.

As a result of the team dashboard's success, Cirrus has begun to develop customer dashboards that track customer and competitor trends for each of their key markets. Here, too, the creation of a measurement system forced people to define what was important rather than merely interesting.

SUMMARY

The most important role that innovation measurement plays is to speed the rate of learning. At its best, a good measurement system warns you of trouble before you ever get there. At the very least, it should provide guidance and enhance coordination.

Left alone, however, today's measurements represent the strongest remaining element of operations thinking. To unleash the true power and passion that knowledge workers bring to innovation, we've got to stop blowing the silent whistle of command and control. The good news is that the tools are here to do so. Between activity-based accounting methodologies and tools that reflect the new knowledge paradigm, such as the dashboard, you can get started *now*.

8

Getting from Here to There

When I'm asked to talk to a group of executives about innovation or cycle time reduction, I always reserve considerable time toward the end for what I call the "so what" discussion: "So, what are you going to do?" That's the focus of this final chapter.

Let's start by retracing our steps. The stage is set by a quick assessment of the changes in the competitive environment. Our conclusion is that a dramatic increase in highly capable global competition, combined with the shift to a knowledge-based economy, demands a renewed emphasis on innovation. Next we explore the world of innovation, and we learn that many of the methods and tools that work so well in managing the daily business don't help here—in fact, they often hurt. We probe what evokes innovative thinking, learn some principles for guiding innovation, and then explore the Innovation System model. Beginning with leadership and management, I have detailed each of the five elements, working counterclockwise to metrics. Now, let's turn to the oval in which all these elements sit—the organization's culture.

CULTURAL OZONE

With regard to air quality, life in the Silicon Valley is much better than in Los Angeles. We take the air we breathe for granted until one of those still, smoggy days reminds us how precious and important it is to our existence. After coughing or wheezing due to the high ozone content, our consciousness is raised, only to fade once more when the sea breeze starts blowing again. In many respects, our relationship with the earth's atmosphere parallels how we respond and care for our companies' cultures, and their impact on innovation.

Just like air, the culture is always there and has a constant impact on innovation, even if we don't see it. When things are going well, culture blends invisibly into the flow of productive activities. It's when things go south that the culture begins to stand out, just as ozone turns colorless air a disturbing shade of greenish-yellow.

What used to work now stands as a barrier to moving forward. Our culture, and the problems we experience with it, become active topics of conversation. Invariably, people talk about wanting to change the culture, but they rarely get specific about what this means in practice. What would they change? What would it take to do that? How long would it require? Could we be successful, or are we caught in some tragic loop where because our culture discourages innovation, the culture itself cannot be changed?

CHANGING THE CULTURE OF INNOVATION

To changing your innovation culture, you must follow the path that California took to reduce air pollution despite a significantly growing population. First, people had to agree that air pollution was a problem worthy of attention. It's easy for us to forget, but environmental activists once were characterized as naive or worse, and rarely as leaders. Only after their concerns were embraced by a critical mass of society did we change our opinions of their worth.

Once opinion started to shift, resources were applied to defining and implementing controls over a broad range of pollution sources. Cars were targeted early, followed by industrial emissions, planes, and eventually aerosol cans. Individual behavior changes came slowly, and rarely without help from a government-defined shift in the cost-benefit equation. The latter began as financial penalties, evolving into a mixture of penalties and public opinion. The time from when the earliest measures were first considered to when the impact could be seen in the skies is appropriately measured in decades.

This may sound frightening, but the point is that culture change requires a broad and *sustained* effort. If you look at the successful culture changes within some of our largest companies, decades are not an unrealistic measurement. General Electric, for example, began aggressively driving for cycle time improvement in the mid-1980s, and they've still got room to go. Similarly, Motorola's efforts for "6 Sigma" quality continue to this day. Even so, you can expect significant benefits along the way.

Simply calling for culture change, though, will have the same impact as asking citizens to use their cars less—that is, none. Forget it. To improve innovation, you have to address the drivers of innovation, just as we attacked the sources of pollutants. That's where our model comes in; it defines the five major drivers. If you focus on changing them, you *will* change your innovation culture.

LEADERS BREAK THE ICE, PRAY, ARCHITECT THE CHANGE, PRAY, POUND THE TABLE, AND PRAY

Another thing that happens whenever I talk to a group of managers about innovation is that someone, usually from a lower rank in the organization, will approach me before I leave and say, "You know who I really wish had been here today . . ." They fill in the blank with the name or title of someone above them—be it their boss, the general manager, or the company president. I've even had a CEO suggest a member of the board of directors!

There's a rich fallacy in many organizations that leaders can force change to happen. It's not true, and it often reflects a troubled person and company. Leaders can and must break the ice for change, but the waters underneath are filled with sharks dressed as middle managers and others, all seeking to retain their power as they define it. There's no question that if the top of the house doesn't set clear goals, allocate resources, and emphasize that this change is personally important to them, the chances of success are slim. At the same time, getting the top people on board only signals the start of the campaign.

Winning that campaign depends on how well the rest of the organization is recruited into the challenge, for performance will only change when the people who do the innovating change their behavior. One of the marvelously ironic aspects of improving your innovation capabilities is that doing so is an innovation itself, with the product being a new innovation delivery capability or service. Because of this, you can use the model itself to help steer the change. For example, let's apply the basic principles of innovation to this challenge:

1. *Strategy should drive innovation.* How does improving innovation fit within your business objectives? What makes participating in this change compelling to your employees, relative to the other demands and plans the business has?
2. *Manage innovation in the aggregate.* Do you have a change strategy for innovation that is congruent with other improvement initiatives? Do you have too many change initiatives on the plate, with the result that none are adequately resourced? Can you envision a "family" of change efforts that create some leverage?
3. *Loose-tight leadership maximizes creativity.* Where do top-down goals and edicts help, and where do you need to evoke ideas and ownership from below? Have you

thought about what could help get things started, compared to how you'll focus energy when the initiative gains momentum?

4. *Broad, multifunctional involvement is essential.* Who should play where and when? Since changing innovation cuts across the entire organization, what is the philosophy and structure you have in mind to ensure this?

5. *Establish a defined, flexible innovation process.* Do you have a change roadmap in mind that defines the steps for getting from here to there? Have you considered managing this with the same rigor and accountability that you would apply to your next-generation platform product or service?

GETTING PERSONAL

One of the challenges you'll face is not just breaking the ice, but having people believe that the ice is indeed broken. Cafeteria speeches and communication sessions are only pump primers. Having watched several organizations go through this process, it's very clear to me what spells the difference between interested and committed. First, far above all else, is how far those who are calling for change go in making visible changes themselves. Talking about the need for the company to change is one thing, but when the people listening see you *acting* differently, then they start believing. If this is a charade, your effort will be labeled "strategy du jour" within a nanosecond.

For yourself, a key question will be where are you spending your time. If changing the innovation capabilities of your organization are important, then you'll spend time strategizing, monitoring, communicating, and (of course) changing how you work. Think back to what Chuck Knight did at Emerson Electric. He created the growth conference, which paralleled the company's longstanding tradition of operations planning conferences. He changed the measurement system. He changed what he asked company presidents to report on, as well as their compensation. In the process, he also shot a couple of sacred cows.

Remember when the company president from the Midwest ran into the masseuse during a benchmark trip to Quantum? In a conversation with him shortly after the visit, we were discussing what it took to make the magnitude of changes that Quantum achieved. His response initially stunned and embarrassed me, but upon reflection I knew he was right. He said he had learned that in addition to all the good strategy, planning, education, and change on the part of many people, the president finally had to "shoot" a couple of senior players who kept undermining the change. He suggested, moreover, that the bodies were left in the equivalent of the town square in order to send a message.

Strong language, but more accurate than not. I recall Jack Welch's letter to General Electric shareholders in this year's annual report, where he revealed that he knew they were serious about change when they were willing to discipline those who got results, but used the old-school approach to do so. Handled promptly, such decisions won't happen often, but rest assured that you will be tested.

GETTING OVER THE LIP TO START

We are marvelously adaptive and reactive creatures. There's no question that people, particularly in the United States, can change. I'd argue that actually we all like change, otherwise the fashion industry would have gone out of business long ago! Our problems with change have much more to do with who has control. When we truly want to change, it's relatively easy. Thus the first step for an innovation improvement is to raise people's awareness about the need for change.

Of the thousand and one ways to raise awareness, two stand out as much more effective than others. The first is to pull the longer-term consequences of continuing today's innovation practices into the present. For example, if your speed or accuracy continues along the same trend line compared to your competitors, what would the impact on your business be? The more you can express this in the traditional lingua franca of market share, profits, and growth, the more effective you'll be. Financial projections can be augmented by case studies from history (where they are available) that parallel your predicament or planned response. Case studies can add a descriptive richness that numbers often lack.

The second and more powerful method is to visit someplace that has successfully made the changes that you are contemplating. One of the reasons that Quantum's leadership was so gracious about hosting visitors from the Midwest is that Quantum's own transformation began with a similar visit for exactly the same purpose.

It doesn't matter how many books you read, courses you attend, or experts you consult with, though—it's hard to be satisfied until you can sit down with a professional peer who's walked the path and ask about what I call the "big worries." Former Quantum president Dave Brown asked his peer if he wasn't scared to death that the whole company might come tumbling down during the change process. When he heard, "Yes, but it didn't happen that way," Brown was ready to change.

WHICH ELEMENT(S) SECOND?

The innovation system has five elements, which suggests that there are five places where you could start. Since I've already illustrated that leadership is a must, there are really only four candidates. We can also eliminate metrics, because they should provide feedback and guide all your efforts but (as described earlier) should not be used to replace goals. That leaves us with strategic alignment, process, and organization and people.

Under certain circumstances, each might be attractive. Of course, many firms tackle more than one at a time. Your decision should be based on your needs and capacity for resourcing and managing change. You can also start work on one element, reach a new plateau, then work on another and come back later to the first. The number of options is endless, so guidelines are more appropriate than explicit advice.

Strategic Alignment

The primary advantage of strategic alignment is that it engages the leadership of the organization from the start. Combined with some education, this puts the leadership team in the front of the organization learning curve. It also provides a chance to clear the development freeway of gridlock and establish clear priorities where those are needed. Trying to improve the development process when it's under tremendous pressure doesn't work.

The primary downside of this approach is threefold. First, its strength is also its weakness: it doesn't involve anyone else. Executive management are not the principal innovation resources, so it doesn't appear that much change is occurring. Second, although the purpose of strategic alignment is strategy definition, resource balancing *and* leverage, early on, the most visible focus is on the resource balancing, and not the leverage. Achieving leverage requires looking at product and service architectures, partnerships, etc., and while that may come up, it normally is not a major consideration this early. Third, while this approach involves management early, if the greatest problems are with the process or people dimension, working on this has little impact.

Process

The advantage of starting with the process is that this is where the data on your innovation practices are the richest; in addition, it intimately involves those who do the work. Executive participation can be orchestrated in the form of sponsorship or steering committees to those examining the process. I have a personal bias toward starting here, even if it's merely a quick postmortem using a process map, because this is where you learn the innovation work requirements. Without those, understanding your capacity and resource requirements is very difficult; plus, if you're going to design a team-function organization, it should be built around the work itself.

The downside of starting with the process is that it's often so cumbersome that understanding and improving it requires a serious commitment. In our consulting practice, going from the old process to a new architecture with accompanying tools can range from three months in a small company to nearly a year in a large one. This timing incorporates all the delays and changes that accompany getting implementation buy-in and commitment. Product innovation projects are lengthy, so you usually want to inaugurate any new process from the start. Certainly, though, trying to introduce a new process into an existing initiative that's past the halfway point should be the exception. With their shorter development times, this is less a problem in service.

Organization and People

Without question, innovation will be hampered significantly until multifunctional work processes become the path of least resistance. If your firm has tall and strong organizational silos, these must be addressed. At the same time, because the change from silos to a multifunctional approach (which combines teams and functions) involves so many people, it is a bear to execute. Chrysler, though, started here. Choose this as your starting point if it's patently clear that your silos are your biggest headache, but make sure you commit major resources and time to making the change successful.

Alternatively, many organizations are using team-function structures today, albeit not as effectively as they could. Since defining that effectiveness is often a soft issue around which there's a great deal of defensiveness, it's often more effective to conduct a postmortem review to see what organization and people issues emerge. At that point, the people who *participate* in the innovation process are defining what's broken, and suggesting the solutions.

SELF-MEDICATION VERSUS OUTSIDE HELP

My experience has significantly changed my thinking about the value of outside help. If you had asked me ten years ago about the role of consultants, my response would have been that companies know their problems far better than any outsiders. Moreover, if they're not willing to lead the change effort, it won't work anyway. I was strongly of the opinion that change had to be led, designed, and managed from within. Why have I changed my thinking?

What I have learned is that very few companies are willing to devote the resources and energy required to drive change on their own. The ability to be persistent and relentless is reserved for the marketplace, not internal improvements; this is particularly true following the years of downsizing. Organizations are now staffed almost exclusively for the core work, with little spare capacity for anything else. Unless the current pain level is very high, adding a major innovation improvement project to someone's plate almost ensures that it will be relegated to the bottom of the list.

Additionally, while there is no question that issues are better known and understood by those inside, people at every level often don't feel free to discuss them—and certainly not with the energy and vigor that they do privately, after work. Today, the most truthful comments are made in restrooms and hallways, usually during meeting breaks. As a consequence, organizations engage in an elusive dance of *rampant pretending*.

Here's how it works. Rampant pretending occurs when the team working on the Atlas initiative knows that although they still have a slight chance, the likelihood of missing the upcoming milestone is very high. They don't say anything officially, though; why get kicked until you have to? Meanwhile, senior managers also have learned that the initiative is running late, but they don't ask the team or say anything either. After all, why destroy their morale if there's still a slim chance? Attempts to drive change under these conditions are rarely successful.

The last factor is breadth of experience. Outside experts who have worked with many firms have had multiple cycles of learning what works and what doesn't. Within any firm, the chances of having anywhere near the same amount of experience are low. Some of the tools described in this book are like golf clubs or tennis racquets—everyone can swing them and hit the ball, but it's only through practice that you can increase the odds that it will go where you want it.

THE FUN FACTOR

Before I close, let me ask you this. Do you really want to know what makes Silicon Valley tick? I mean deep inside, at the core?

The truth is . . . it's a ball! Hard work combined with hard play—at every level, from executive down and back up again. When I return from traveling around the world to help others learn innovation, I'm always struck not only by how hard people in the Valley work, but also by how much fun they are having at the same time. On closer examination, they are not just having fun, but planning it and making it part of the culture. This is the spirit that truly enables relentless innovation.

Notes

Introduction

1. Annalee Saxenian, *Regional Advantage: Culture and Competition in Silicon Valley and Route 128* (Cambridge: Harvard University Press, 1994), p. 2.
2. Annalee Saxenian, *Regional Advantage: Culture and Competition in Silicon Valley and Route 128* (Cambridge: Harvard University Press, 1994), p. 2.
3. Ian Morrison and Greg Schmid, *Future Tense: The Business Realities of the Next Ten Years* (New York: William Morrow & Company), p. 171–172.
4. Cisco's acquisition of StrataCom works because StrataCom keeps growing.

Chapter 1

1. John Huey, "Waking Up to the New Economy," *Fortune*, June 6, 1994, p. 36–46.
2. Thomas A. Stewart, "Welcome to the Revolution," *Fortune*, December 13, 1993, p. 66.
3. *Economist*, "Multinationals," p. 5–6.
4. Michael Polanyi, *The Tacit Dimension* (London: Routledge & Kegan Paul), p. 26.
5. Ian Morrison and Greg Schmid, *Future Tense: The Business Realities of the Next Ten Years* (New York: William Morrow & Company), p. 77.
6. Ian Morrison and Greg Schmid, *Future Tense: The Business Realities of the Next Ten Years* (New York: William Morrow & Company), p. 84.
7. Rebecca Henderson, "Managing Innovation in the Information Age," *Harvard Business Review*, p. 102.

8. James E. Ellis, "Why Overseas? 'Cause That's Where the Sales Are," *Business Week*, January 10, 1994.
9. *Economist*, "Management Focus: Producer Power," March 4, 1995, p. 70.
10. Saul Hansell, "The Ante Rises in East Asia," *The New York Times*, July 14, 1996.
11. Ian Morrison and Greg Schmid, *Future Tense: The Business Realities of the Next Ten Years* (New York: William Morrow & Company), p. 81–82.
12. Conversation with Mr. Tim Solso, COO, Cummins Engine Company, Columbus, Indiana.
13. Sylvia Nasar, "The American Economy, Back on Top," *The New York Times*, February, 27, 1994, p. 1f.
14. Sylvia Nasar, "The American Economy, Back on Top," *The New York Times*, February, 27, 1994, p. 1f.
15. John Huey, "Waking Up to the New Economy," *Fortune*, June 6, 1994, p. 36–46.
16. Sylvia Nasar, "The American Economy, Back on Top," *The New York Times*, February, 27, 1994, p. 1f.
17. Paula Dwyer, Pete Engardio, Zachary Schiller and Stanley Reed, "Tearing Up Today's Organization Chart," *Business Week*, November 14, 1995, p. 80–90.

Chapter 2

1. Syntex Corporation, "Facts About Your Industry," *Syntex—Public Affairs and Communications*, Palo Alto, California, July, 1990.
2. Pharmecutical Research and Manufacturers of America, "New Drug Approvals in 1994," January, 1995.
3. Brain O'Reilly, "Ideas and New Products," *Fortune*, March 3, 1997, p. 60.
4. Conversation with Professor Ralph Katz, Massachusetts Institute of Technology, 1996.
5. Conversation with Professor Ralph Katz, Massachusetts Institute of Technology, 1996.
6. Donald Reinertson and Preston Smith, *Developing Products in Half the Time*, (New York: Van Nostrand Reinhold, 1991), p. 43.

Chapter 3

1. Conversation with David Pottruck, President of Charles R. Schwab, Inc. San Francisco, California, March, 1996.
2. Speech by Gary Hamel, Emerson Electric Company, St. Louis, November 1996.
3. Paul Stonham, "The Future of Strategy: An Interview with Gary Hamel," *European Management Journal*, June, 1993, p. 150–157.
4. Charles F. Knight, "Emerson Electric: Consistent Profits, Consistently," *Harvard Business Review*, January–February, 1992, p. 57–70.

Chapter 4

1. Donald Reinertson and Preston Smith, *Developing Products in Half the Time* (New York: Van Nostrand Reinhold, 1991), p. 43.
2. Elliott Jaques, *Requisite Organization* (Arlington, Virginia: Carson Hall, 1989), p. 50.
3. Michael Porter, "What is Strategy," *The Harvard Business Review*, p. 61.
4. Steven C. Wheelwright and Kim B. Clark, *Revolutionizing Product Development* (New York: Free Press, 1992), p. 95.
5. Steven C. Wheelwright and Kim B. Clark, *Revolutionizing Product Development* (New York: Free Press, 1992), p. 93.

Chapter 5

1. David Bank, "The Java Saga," *Wired*, December, 1995.
2. Steven C. Wheelwright and Kim B. Clark, *Revolutionizing Product Development* (New York: Free Press, 1992), p. 119.
3. Marco Iansiti, "Shooting the Rapids: Managing Product Development in Turbulent Environments, *California Management Review*, Volume 38, Number 1, Fall, 1995.
4. Marco Iansiti, "Shooting the Rapids: Managing Product Development in Turbulent Environments, *California Management Review*, Volume 38, Number 1, Fall, 1995.

Chapter 6

1. Jonno Hanafin, Long Valley, New Jersey, first introduced this concept to me while at Exxon Chemicals in 1979.
2. Homa Bahrami, "The Emerging Flexible Organization: Perspectives from Silicon Valley," *California Management Review*, Volume 34, Number 54, Summer, 1992.
3. Alan Deutschman, "The Managing Wisdom of High-Tech Superstars," *Fortune*, October 17, 1994, p. 197–206.
4. Alan Deutschman, "The Managing Wisdom of High-Tech Superstars," *Fortune*, October 17, 1994, p. 197–206.
5. Carrie Gottlieb, "Intel's Plan for Staying on Top," *Fortune*, March 27, 1989, p. 98–100.
6. Thanks for this view of Quantum Corporation, Milpitas, California, which comes from Jane Creech, Human Resources Director.
7. For further information, see Christopher Meyer, *Fast Cycle Time* (New York: Free Press, 1993) chapter 5.
8. Tracy Kidder, *Soul of a New Machine* (New York: Little Brown, 1981)
9. Brian Dumaine, "Why Do We Work?" *Fortune*, December 26, 1994, p. 196–204.

Chapter 7

1. Christopher Meyer, *Fast Cycle Time* (New York: Free Press, 1993).
2. Christopher Meyer, "How the Right Measures Help Teams Excel," *Harvard Business Review*, May–June, 1994.
3. Christopher Meyer, "How the Right Measures Help Teams Excel," *Harvard Business Review*, May–June, 1994, and Robert Kaplan and David Norton, "Putting the Balanced Scorecard to Work," *Harvard Business Review*, September–October, 1993.
4. Tony Hope and Jeremy Hope, *Transforming the Bottom Line* (London: Nicholas Brealey, 1995)
5. Chris Argyris, "Good Communication that Blocks Learning," *Harvard Business Review*, July–August, 1994.
6. Christopher Meyer, "How the Right Measures Help Teams Excel," *Harvard Business Review*, May–June, 1994.

Index

About the Author

Christopher Meyer is Managing Principal of Integral, Inc., a management consulting firm that specializes in technology and innovation management, operations enhancement, and competitive strategy. Dr. Meyer is an internationally recognized expert in new product and service development, with an emphasis on technology-market strategy, cycle time reduction, development process improvement and performance measurement. He teaches executives at Stanford University and the California Institute of Technology-Industrial Relations Center. Prior to leading Integral, he was the founder of the Strategic Alignment Group and has served as an executive at Silicon Graphics Computer Systems, Zilog and Exxon Chemicals, as well as on the faculty of the University of Minnesota and the University of Southern California.

Blending nearly thirty years experience as an executive, consultant and researcher, Dr. Meyer is also the author of *Fast Cycle Time* (Free Press, 1993). His current interest is distilling the practical implications of best of breed innovation practices, as discovered by industry, with the latest advances in management research, technology, and business strategy. He works out of Integral's Menlo Park, California office, and can be reached via email at cmeyer@Integral-Inc.com.